W0317311

A BELIEVER'S GUIDE TO FASTING

Two Treatises on the Rulings, Merits and Secrets of Fasting

SECOND EDITION

ʿABD-ALLĀH SIRĀJ AL-DĪN
& MUḤAMMAD HISHĀM BURHĀNĪ

Translated & Annotated by
Amjad Mahmood

HERITAGE PRESS

A Believer's Guide to Fasting

Published by: Heritage Press
First Edition published in: June 2013 / Shaʿbān 1434
Second Edition published in: May 2014 / Rajab 1435
Reprinted in: February 2024 / Shaʿbān 1445
Website: www.heritagepress.co.uk
E-mail: info@heritagepress.co.uk

Authors: Shaykh ʿAbd-Allāh Sirāj al-Dīn and Shaykh Hishām Burhānī
Translated by: Amjad Mahmood

A CIP catalogue record for this book is available with the British Library

ISBN: 978-0-9576937-4-6

Typeset by: Mohammed Almass and Faisal Hussain
Cover Design by: Qutaiba al-Mahawili

A BELIEVER'S GUIDE TO FASTING

Two Treatises on the Rulings, Merits and Secrets of Fasting

CONTENTS

Treatise Two · *Al-Ṣawm*

SHAYKH MUḤAMMAD HISHĀM BURHĀNĪ

TRANSLITERATION KEY

ء	ʾ (A distinctive glottal stop made at the bottom of the throat.)
ا	*a, a*
ب	*b*
ت	*t*
ث	*th* (Pronounced like the *th* in think.)
ج	*j*
ح	*ḥ* (Hard *h* sound made at the Adam's apple in the middle of the throat.)
خ	*kh* (Pronounced like the *ch* in Scottish loch.)
د	*d*
ذ	*dh* (Pronounced like the *th* in this.)
ر	*r*
ز	*z*
س	*s*
ش	*sh*
ص	*ṣ* (An emphatic *s* pronounced behind the upper front teeth.)
ض	*ḍ* (An emphatic *d*-like sound made by pressing the entire tongue against the upper palate.)
ط	*ṭ* (An emphatic *t* pronounced behind the front teeth.)
ظ	*ẓ* (An emphatic *th*, like the th in this, made behind the front teeth.)
ع	ʿ (A distinctive Semitic sound made in the middle of the throat, sounding to a Western ear more like a vowel than a consonant.)
غ	*gh* (A guttural sound made at the top of the throat, resembling the untrilled German and French *r*.)
ف	*f*
ق	*q* (A guttural *k* sound produced at the back of the palate.)
ك	*k*
ل	*l*
م	*m*
ن	*n*
ه	*h*
و	*w, u, ū*
ي	*y, i, ī*

TRANSLATOR'S INTRODUCTION

In the name of Allah, the All-merciful, the Compassionate. May Allah's blessings be upon our master Muhammad, the master of all messengers and the seal of all prophets, the one who said, 'For whomsoever Allah wills good, He grants him deep understanding (*fiqh*) of the religion,' and upon his family, Companions and those who follow them with excellence until the Day of Judgement.

Before the reader is a translation of two short treatises, which were originally penned in Arabic on the subject of fasting by two eminent scholars of Syria. The first of these is by the late erudite scholar and gnostic from Aleppo, Syria, Shaykh ʿAbd-Allāh Sirāj al-Dīn al-Ḥusaynī - may Allah be well-pleased with him - entitled *Al-Ṣiyām* (Fasting). The second, *Al-Ṣawm* (*ṣawm* being a synonym of *ṣiyām*), is by the contemporary scholar of Damascus Shaykh Hishām Burhānī, a specialist in the Ḥanafī school of jurisprudence and a spiritual master of the Shādhilī Sufi way. It was written by the author under the supervision of two of the foremost Ḥanafī jurists of Syria of their time Shaykh ʿAbd al-Wahhāb 'Dibs wa Zayt' and Shaykh Muḥammad Saʿīd Burhānī, which is why their biographies have been included in the current translation.

The first of these treatises examines the virtues, benefits, requirements and etiquette of fasting, paying greater attention to the fasting of Ramadan. However, it does not delve into the legal aspects pertaining to fasting, which is the primary focus of the second treatise that details the external rulings of fasting according to the Ḥanafī school, though also includes a short chapter on the secrets and wisdom behind fasting. Footnotes have been added wherever necessary to aid readers unfamiliar with books of Islamic jurisprudence.

And not forgetting the words of the Prophet ﷺ 'Whosoever is ungrateful to people, is ungrateful to Allah', I would like to express my gratitude to Uthman Ali for his support throughout the translation, especially in providing transliteration for Arabic names and terms, footnotes and part-translation of the first treatise. I would also like to extend my gratitude to Muhammad Ridwaan for expending his valuable time in copy-editing the work and Mohammed Almass and Faisal Hussain for typesetting it; may Allah Most High generously reward them all.

SHAYKH 'ABD-ALLĀH SIRĀJ AL-DĪN AL-ḤUSAYNĪ

He was born in 1343/1924, into a family of knowledge and piety, wherein he was nurtured by his righteous father, Shaykh Muḥammad Najīb Sirāj al-Dīn, who was at the time, one of the foremost scholars of Qur'anic exegesis (*tafsīr*), hadith, Islamic jurisprudence (*fiqh*) and Sufism in Aleppo, and was given the epithet 'Reviver of the Sunnah'. He began his Islamic studies at an early age under the supervision of his father, memorised the Qur'an by the age of thirteen, and would also attend his father's lessons. He enrolled at the Khuṣrawiyyah institute of Islamic learning, regarded at the time as the 'al-Azhar' of Syria. There he studied for the next several years under the leading scholars of Aleppo, such as Shaykh Muḥammad Ibrāhīm al-Silqīnī, the mufti of Aleppo Shaykh Aḥmad al-Kurdī, the hadith specialist (*muḥaddith*) and historian Shaykh Rāghib al-Ṭabbākh and many other luminaries. His teachers were mesmerised by the sharpness of his intellect and his capacity for learning, invariably the top student in all subjects and surpassing many students that were senior to him. He would devote his summer holidays for memorisation of hadiths, eventually memorising all those contained in the six books of hadith (*al-kutub al-sittah*). One of his most senior students and son-in-law, Shaykh Nūr al-Dīn 'Itr, estimates that he memorised eighty thousand hadiths; thus he was conferred the epithet of '*al-Ḥāfiẓ*', whilst Shaykh

Nūr al-Dīn also deems him 'deserving of the title "Shaykh al-Islām" as he mastered the major Islamic sciences'.

After the completion of his studies at the Khuṣrawiyyah institute he continued studying advanced works in the various Islamic sciences such as the *Ḥāshiyah Ibn ʿĀbidīn*, the foremost authoritative work in the Ḥanafī school of jurisprudence, under the supervision of his father. He began to teach in various mosques across Aleppo, including the Umayyad Mosque, after which he was asked to teach at numerous institutes, amongst them the Shaʿbāniyyah Islamic school. At the age of twenty-two he was tasked with taking over his father's lessons at various mosques due to the latter's old age.

In 1958 after the closure of the Shaʿbāniyyah school, he established the School of Islamic Learning, where all the Islamic sciences were taught. It was not long before Shaykh ʿAbd-Allāh became the leading scholarly authority of Aleppo, having memorised approximately eighty thousand hadiths, and being a prominent exegete of the Qur'an, as demonstrated by his works on the exegesis of various chapters of the Qur'an. However, he was most famously known for his deep love and attachment to the Messenger of Allah ﷺ about whose qualities, characteristics, elevated status and love he never ceased to speak about in his lessons, private and public, and in his literary works too. He would constantly remind people of the sublime qualities of the Messenger of Allah ﷺ and the obligation to love and follow him. This was clearly manifested in his acclaimed work *Our Master Muhammad the Messenger of Allah: His Sublime Character and Exalted Attributes*, which was recently translated into the English language. Some of his students mentioned that he would be visited by the Messenger of Allah ﷺ both in sleep and when awake. He was scrupulous in all of his affairs as attested to by Shaykh Nūr al-Dīn ʿItr, who said about him, 'He would personally follow the most stringent ruling on matters, within the four schools of jurisprudence, whilst issuing the more lenient verdict of the four schools to laymen.'

He authored over twenty works on a wide range of subjects such as Islamic ethics, spirituality, Qur'anic exegesis, tenets of faith and the prophetic characteristics. He left behind many students who later became prominent scholars in their own right, such as his son Shaykh Aḥmad Yaḥyā Sirāj al-Dīn, his son-in-law and nephew Shaykh Nūr al-Dīn ʿItr, Shaykh Muḥammad ʿAwwāmah, Shaykh Wahbī al-Ghawjī and many others. He passed unto his Lord on 4 March 2002.[1]

---

1 Biographical notes taken from ʿItr, Nūr al-Dīn. *Ṣafaḥāt min ḥayāh al-Imām Shaykh al-Islām al-Shaykh ʿAbd-Allāh Sirāj al-Dīn al-Ḥusaynī*. Damascus: Dār al-Ru'yah, 1423/2002.

SHAYKH MUḤAMMAD HISHĀM BURHĀNĪ

Born in Damascus in 1932, he accompanied his father Shaykh Muḥammad Saʿīd Burhānī from a young age and through his father he thus became acquainted with the greatest scholars of that era. He would meet and attend the gatherings of some of the most eminent scholars, including: Shaykh ʿAbd al-Qādir al-Askandarānī, Shaykh Ṣāliḥ al-Ḥimṣī, Shaykh Maḥmūd Saʿīd al-Ḥamzāwī and others. He drank a great deal from the spring of his father and those of his contemporaries, such as Shaykh Abū al-Khayr al-Maydānī and Shaykh ʿAbd al-Wahhāb al-Ḥāfiẓ (better known as 'Dibs wa Zayt'), Shaykh Muḥammad al-Hāshimī, the shaykh of his father, Shaykh Ḥasan al-Ḥabannakah, Shaykh al-Makkī al-Kattānī, Shaykh Ṣāliḥ al-Farfūr, Shaykh ʿAbd al-Razzāq al-Ḥalabī and Shaykh Adīb Kallās. He studied the sacred sciences and the ancillary disciplines during various stages throughout his scholarly pursuits.

In 1952, he began memorising the Qur'an with the jurist of Damascus and specialist Qur'an reciter Shaykh ʿAbd al-Wahhāb 'Dibs wa Zayt', under whose tutelage he completed it. He graduated from the faculty of shariah at the University of Damascus in the academic year 1958–59. His lecturers included: Shaykh Aḥmad Fahmī Abū Sunnah, Shaykh Muḥammad Muntaṣir al-Kattānī, Shaykh Muṣṭafā Zarqā and Shaykh Abū al-Yusr ʿĀbidīn. During his studies at the faculty, he would teach at the Dār al-Ḥadīth institute when Shaykh Maḥmūd Rankūsī was its principle. Following his graduation, he was appointed a teacher in secondary schools in Swaydāʾ, and then later transferred as assistant lecturer in the faculty of shariah at the University of Damascus in 1959–60. In 1961 he travelled to Egypt to continue further studies at Dār al-ʿUlūm in Cairo from where he attained an MA in Islamic law with a distinction. He returned to Damascus in 1968 as a teacher and later as a lecturer in the faculty of shariah, teaching jurisprudence (*fiqh*), legal theory (*uṣūl al-fiqh*) and Qur'anic exegesis (*tafsīr*). He represented the Emirates during the 1980s in various roles at the Islamic Jurisprudence Council in Jeddah for several years.

He would teach publicly in the Grand Umayyad and Tawbah Mosques, in the fields of jurisprudence, prophetic biography (*sīrah*) and Sufism (*taṣawwuf*). Amongst the works he authored are his MA thesis entitled *Sadd al-dharāʾiʿ* [Curtailing the pre-texts], *ʿIlm tajwīd al-Qurʾān*, and a series of epistles in Islamic worship including the present work. He passed away on 27 April 2014 in Damascus at the age of 82.

SHAYKH MUḤAMMAD SAʿĪD BURHĀNĪ

A Ḥanafī jurist and Shādhilī Sufi master. He was born in Damascus 1311/1892. His great-grandfather migrated to Damascus from Dagestan and settled there. At the end of the First World War, in 1918, he joined the Ottoman army from which he was later given leave to complete his scholarly pursuits. He then joined the Arab Syrian army after the establishment of the Arab state in Syria, holding the position of reserve officer. And when the French attacked Damascus, he was one of the first to join the Syrian army position in Maysalūn.

He later began teaching in various schools in villages until he finally settled in Damascus. He initially studied under his father, followed by: Shaykh ʿAbd al-Qādir al-Askandarānī, the Greatest Hadith Master Shaykh Badr al-Dīn al-Ḥasanī, the mufti of Syria Shaykh ʿAṭāʾ Allāh al-Kasam, and Shaykh Abū al-Khayr al-Maydānī from whom he also took the Naqshabandī order prior to becoming a disciple of Shaykh al-Sayyid Muḥammad al-Hāshimī. In 1932, following the loss of his father, he took over teaching his lessons in the Tawbah Mosque. Upon his retirement in 1945, he dedicated himself to teaching and inviting others to the Sufi way after being authorised as a *murshid* (spiritual guide) during the lifetime of his Shaykh. He was made his successor and would, therefore, cover for his Shaykh's lessons during his absence. He was also authorised by many scholars, such as Shaykh Badr al-Dīn al-Ḥasanī and Shaykh Maḥmūd al-ʿAṭṭār.

He stood out in humility, purity of heart, maintaining good opinion of others and remaining in constant remembrance of Allah. He was abstinent from the world and loved the friends of Allah. Along with Shaykh ʿĀrif ʿUthmān, he established the gatherings devoted to invoking blessings upon the Prophet ﷺ in numerous cities within Syria. He edited, annotated and prepared indexes for numerous works including his acclaimed edition of the book *al-Hadiyyah al-ʿAlāʾiyyah* [The Gift of ʿAlāʾ]—considered an abridgement of the authoritative work in Ḥanafī jurisprudence *Ḥāshiyah* of Ibn ʿĀbidīn—written by his son ʿAlāʾ al-Din ʿĀbidīn, and *al-Durar al-mubāḥah*, an authoritative Ḥanafī work on halal and haram, as well as many of his own Shaykh's works including a number of manuscripts and concise epistles in various sciences yet to be published. He passed away in 1387/1967.[2]

---

2 Biographical notes taken from ʿĀbidīn, ʿAlāʾ al-Din. *al-Hadiyyah al-ʿAlāʾiyyah*. 5th edn. Damascus: n.p., 1416/1995.

SHAYKH ʿABD AL-WAHHĀB DIBS WA ZAYT

A jurist of the Ḥanafīs, *ḥāfiẓ* and *muqri'* (a specialist Qur'anic instructor), ʿAbd al-Wahhāb ʿAbd al-Raḥīm ibn ʿAbd-Allāh ibnʿAbd al-Qādir ibn ʿAbd al-Wahhāb al-Ḥāfiẓ, better known as 'Dibs wa Zayt'. His lineage returns back to the illustrious saint Shaykh ʿAbd al-Qādir al-Jīlānī. The epithet Ḥāfiẓ is with reference to the many members of the family who had memorised the Qur'an.

Born in the year 1311/1892, he memorised the Qur'an with his father at a young age. He studied with Shaykh Amīn Suwayd legal theory (*uṣūl al-fiqh*) and Sufism (*taṣawwuf*), and also read uṣūl al-fiqh, Arabic language and Islamic theology with Shaykh Maḥmūd al-ʿAṭṭār. He adhered to the lessons of Shaykh Badr al-Dīn al-Ḥasanī and had a very close relationship with him, such that the latter allocated study times exclusively for him. He also studied with Shaykh ʿAbd al-Qādir al-Askandarānī, Shaykh Ṣāliḥ al-Ḥimṣī, and met the likes of Shaykh Salīm al-Masūtī and Shaykh ʿAbd al-Ḥakīm al-Afghānī. He took the Naqshabandī order from Shaykh ʿĪsā al-Kurdī; many scholarly discussions took place between the two where Shaykh ʿĪsā realised his acumen and deep understanding of the sacred texts and derivation of rulings, such that he said to him on one occasion, 'Devote yourself to *fiqh*, my son.' The most influential of his teachers was the mufti of the Levant Shaykh Muḥammad ʿAṭā' Allāh al-Kasam, who noticed his unique, prodigious talent and thus gifted him his personal copy of *Ḥāshiyah* of Ibn ʿĀbidīn, which he studied three times with the shaykh, once from the chapter of 'Renting and Hiring' to the end, and twice more from beginning to end. Shaykh Muḥammad ʿAṭā' was his principle teacher; he would attend all his lessons, private and public, never leaving him except for the night of his wedding, for which he was later reproached. He named him his successor (*khalīfah*) after him and nicknamed him 'Abū Ḥanīfah Junior'. He received three *ijāzah*s (authorisations) from Shaykh Badr al-Dīn al-Ḥasanī, Shaykh Muḥammad ʿAṭā' Allāh al-Kasam and Shaykh Muḥammad Riḍwān, the scholar of al-Madīnah al-Munawwarah, from whom he received an authorisation in *Dalā'il al-khayrāt* of which Shaykh Muḥammad Riḍwān was a renowned authority.

His mannerisms resembled that of the earliest generations of Muslims; hence he would renounce the world and suffice himself with little, and was scrupulous in matters of halal and haram and would not accept the invitations of many except those of his sincere companions, and of whom he was certain their food was from a halal source. He refused many positions of authority such as becoming General Mufti and the imam of the Grand Umayyad Mosque. He had deep love for the Messenger ﷺ and thus would visit Medina and be eager to perform the pilgrimage to Mecca every year, which he continued up until three years prior to his death. He had great love for the *awliyā'* (friends of Allah) and would thus regularly visit their graves, especially that of Shaykh Muḥyī al-Dīn ibn 'Arabī and Shaykh Arsalān al-Dimashqī, as well as those of his parents and teachers. He gave public lessons in many mosques, including the Grand Umayyad Mosque, and private lessons at his own home and those of his friends. He was a member of the Scholars' League headed by Shaykh Abū al-Khayr al-Maydānī, and the foremost authority in fatwa. Letters flooded in from all over the Muslim world seeking his legal verdicts; he would adopt stringency in all his affairs as he also did in issuing fatwas, and would do so according to the most authoritative opinion in the school of Imam

Abū Ḥanīfah on any given issue and avoid issuing dispensations or weaker opinions.

His devotion to teaching and issuing fatwas meant he spent little time in producing literary works, though he authored a short treatise entitled *Hidāyah al-Raḥmān fī tajwīd ʿilm al-Qurʾān*, a primer on Qur'anic rules of recitation which received great acceptance in scholarly circles, and many students today not only study the work but also commit it to memory. In addition, he also supervised the production of the series of short epistles on Islamic worship written by Shaykh Hishām Burhānī. His students were later to become among the greatest luminaries of the following generation of scholars and include the late mufti of both the Ḥanafīs and Mālikīs in the Levant Shaykh Ibrāhīm al-Yaʿqūbī, Shaykh Asʿad al-Ṣāgharjī and many others.[3]

---

3 Biographical notes taken from al-Ḥāfiẓ, Muḥammad Muṭīʿ. *Taʾrīkh ʿulamāʾ Dimashq*. Damascus: Dār al-Fikr, 1406/1986, 2:829.

Treatise One

Al-Ṣiyām

SHAYKH ʿABD-ALLĀH SIRĀJ AL-DĪN AL-ḤUSAYNĪ

بسم الله الرحمن الرحيم

AUTHOR'S REQUEST

Dear noble reader—

Recite *Sūrah al-Fātiḥah* whenever you read any of my books and gift its reward to the erudite scholar (*al-ʿallāmah*), the great gnostic, the flag-bearer of proof from the Book [Qur'an] and the Sunnah, the Qur'anic exegete and hadith scholar—with connected chains of transmission from the greatest hadith scholars (*muḥaddithīn*) of Aleppo, Damascus, Morocco and other Islamic countries, and authorisations that are elevated in their chains of transmission that are preserved with me—my master, my shaykh and noble father Shaykh Muḥammad Najīb Sirāj al-Dīn al-Ḥusaynī. May Allah Most High have mercy on him and reward him well on behalf of the Muslims, for verily He is the All-hearing, the All-knowing.

Āmīn.

AUTHOR'S INTRODUCTION

All praise belongs to Allah, the Lord of the Worlds. May His blessings and peace be upon our master Muhammad, the Seal of all Prophets, and upon his family and Companions.

To proceed: this concise treatise, albeit hastily compiled, discusses some of the virtues of fasting, its etiquette, requirements, benefits and fruits, through which the ignorant learns, the heedless is reminded and the intelligent reflects. I wanted to expound unequivocally on the topics and sufficiently clarify the rulings of fasting therein—except that I was unable to due to time constraints, so I have partially collated some of that, so that perhaps Allah Most High may enable me to be more exhaustive in the second edition. Surely, my Lord is the answerer of supplications and the fulfiller of hopes.

CHAPTER ONE
The Legislation of Fasting

THE UNIVERSAL LEGISLATION OF FASTING FOR ALL NATIONS

Allah Most High said: '*O you who believe, fasting has been prescribed for you, as it was prescribed for those before you, that you may become God-conscious.*' (Qur'an 2:183)

This noble verse demonstrates that fasting is a universal legislation, for this [Muhammadan] nation and all nations before it. No divinely revealed law was devoid of it, for it is of fundamental interest to mankind, and a lofty degree of perfection. We are guided to this wisdom by the Most High's words '*that you may become God-conscious*', that is to say, perhaps you may attain by your fasting the degrees of *taqwā* (God-consciousness) that consist of impenetrable barriers of protection: protection for the body from ailments, protection for the limbs from carnal desires, protection for the mind and thoughts from doubts, and protection for the heart from Satanic whisperings and [preoccupation with] other than Allah—just as some of that will be made clear if Allah Most High wills.

That which demonstrates the obligation to fast for all divinely revealed laws is the hadith narrated by al-Tirmidhī on the authority of al-Ḥārith al-Ashʿarī ﷺ, that the Messenger of Allah ﷺ said:

> Allah Most Blessed and High commanded Yaḥyā, the son of Zakariyyā (peace be upon them both), with five commandments that he was to carry out and order the Children of Israel to do. So he gathered the people in the Sacred House [in Jerusalem] until it was full, and they sat upon raised platforms. He then said, 'Allah Most High has commanded me with five commandments that you and I must carry out. The first of them is that you worship Allah and not associate anything with Him. Verily, the example of one who associates others with Allah is like that of a man who buys a slave solely of his own wealth with gold or silver and then says, "Here is my home and work, so toil and render [the fruits of your labour] to me." But he would work and render [them] to someone other than his master. Who amongst you would be pleased to have such a slave?!
>
> Allah Most High has commanded you to pray, so when you do so, do not look away, for Allah turns His countenance towards the face of His slave in prayer as long as he does not look away.
>
> He has commanded you to fast, for verily the similitude of that is like that of a man within a group who has with him a pouch in which there is musk, and so all of them are impressed with its fragrance. Surely, the fragrance of the one fasting is more pleasant to Allah than the fragrance of musk.
>
> He has commanded you to give charity, for the similitude of that is like that of a man who is captured by the enemy, and then they fetter his two hands to his neck and bring him forth to behead him. So he says, "I ransom him [meaning himself] from you with everything I possess", and ransoms himself from them.
>
> He has commanded you to remember Allah Most High, since the similitude of that is like that of a man being swiftly pursued by the enemy, until he reaches an impenetrable fortress and so guards himself against them. So too the slave does not guard himself against Satan except by remembering Allah Most High.'

Thus, fasting is legislated in the sacred laws of Allah Most High; however, they differ with regard to its number and period. In some divine laws, perpetual fasting was made incumbent as has been related about the law of Nūḥ ﷺ, and that was commensurate with their robust bodies. In some laws, the fast of fifty days was made incumbent, and so forth. In this manner, the number and periods varied according to the disparity, capacities and potentials.

Allah has made it incumbent upon this Muhammadan nation—the best of nations—to fast the best month of the year; and that is the month of Ramadan. This is the most perfect legislation for fasting and the best decree for the benefit of mankind.

Al-Bazzār narrates on the authority of Abū Saʿīd ﷺ, who ascribed (*marfūʿ*)[10] back to the Prophet ﷺ, 'The pre-eminent month is the month of Ramadan, and the most sacred of them is Dhū al-Ḥijjah.'

Al-Ṭabarānī narrates on the authority of ʿAbd-Allāh ibn Masʿūd ﷺ that he said, 'The leader of the months is the month of Ramadan, and the leader of the days is Friday.'

THE OBLIGATION TO FAST THE MONTH OF RAMADAN

Allah Most High said: '*The month of Ramadan in which the Qur'an was revealed, as a guidance for mankind, and clear signs of [His] guidance, and the criterion [between right and wrong]. So whoever amongst you witnesses [the new moon], then let him fast the month ...*' (Qur'an 2:185)

It is related in the *Ṣaḥīḥ*[11] of al-Bukhārī from Anas ﷺ who said, 'While we were sitting with the Prophet ﷺ in the mosque, a man on a camel entered, knelt it down in the mosque, tied it and said to them, "Who amongst you is Muhammad ﷺ?" We replied, "This fair man who is reclining." The man then said, "The son of ʿAbd al-Muṭṭalib?" The Prophet ﷺ said, "I have answered you." So the man said to the Prophet ﷺ, "I will ask you sternly so do not get upset with me." He ﷺ replied, "Ask whatever is on your mind." So

---

[10] A technical hadith term used to describe a narration by a Companion attributing a statement, action or quality directly to the Prophet ﷺ.

[11] The name commonly used to refer to the hadith collection of Imam al-Bukhārī, accepted as containing the most rigorously authenticated narrations, and is included amongst the six hadith collections (*al-kutub al-sittah*).

he said, "I ask you by your Lord and the Lord of those before you, did Allah send you to the whole of mankind?" He ﷺ replied, "By Allah, yes." He said, "I implore you by Allah Most High, did Allah command you to perform the five prayers by day and night?" He ﷺ replied, "By Allah, yes." He said, "I implore you by Allah Most High, did Allah command you to fast this month of the year?" He ﷺ replied, "By Allah, yes." He said, "I implore you by Allah Most High, did Allah command you to take these alms from our wealthy and distribute them amongst our poor?" He ﷺ replied, "By Allah, yes." So the man said: "I have believed in whatever you have brought."'

The Prophet ﷺ regarded the fasting of Ramadan as one of the pillars of Islam, for he said, 'Islam is built upon five: testifying that there is no god besides Allah and that Muhammad is His slave and messenger, establishing the prayer, giving zakat, making the pilgrimage to the House and fasting Ramadan.' (Agreed upon [by al-Bukhārī and Muslim])

WARNING AGAINST NEGLECTING THE FASTING OF RAMADAN WITHOUT A VALID EXCUSE

There has come a stern warning and an emphatic threat in the prophetic Sunnah for whomsoever breaks the fast of Ramadan without a [valid] dispensation: travel, illness and the like.

Al-Tirmidhī, Abū Dāwūd and al-Nasā'ī narrate on the authority of Abū Hurayrah ؓ that the Messenger of Allah ﷺ said, 'Whoever breaks the fast of a day in Ramadan without a dispensation or illness, then his fasting [perpetually] for an entire lifetime would not compensate for it, even if he were to fast it.'

The scholars have said: what is meant here is that he does not attain the merit of Ramadan, nor does he achieve its purity and divinely bestowed blessing (*barakah*), even though he will be absolved of [the fast of] that day by making it up and atoning, which the Lawgiver has made incumbent wherever it is necessary.

CHAPTER TWO
The Etiquette of Fasting

INTRODUCTION

It behoves the one fasting to restrain his tongue and the rest of his limbs from unlawful acts and sins, so that the meaning of fasting, which is restraint, is realised.

It has come in the *Ṣaḥīḥayn*[12] (the wording is that of al-Bukhārī) on the authority of Abū Hurayrah ﷺ that the Messenger of Allah ﷺ said: 'Fasting is a shield, so do not speak obscenely nor behave ignorantly [with foul deeds]. If an individual fights or abuses one, let him say, "I am fasting, I am fasting." By Him in whose hand is my soul, certainly the breath from the mouth of the one fasting is more pleasant to Allah than the fragrance of musk.'

Al-Bukhārī also narrated on the authority of Abū Hurayrah ﷺ that the Messenger of Allah ﷺ said, 'Whoever does not abstain from false allegation and acting in accordance with it, then [know] that Allah is in no need[13] of him abandoning his food and drink.'

---

12 Referring to the two hadith collections by Imams al-Bukhārī and Muslim, accepted as the most authentic of all collections.

13 Allah is without need of anything, and is never in need of the actions of His own creation. Thus, the reference to 'need' in the hadith is purely an expression of Allah's rejection of his fast.

It is related on the authority of Abū Hurayrah that the Messenger of Allah ﷺ said, 'Many a person fasting does not gain anything from his fast except hunger, and many a person standing [in prayer] does not gain anything from his standing except sleeplessness.' (Narrated by Ibn Mājah, whose wording it is, al-Nasā'ī and others.)

Al-Nasā'ī narrated with an authentic (*ḥasan*) chain of transmission, as did al-Ṭabarānī, whose wording it is, that the Prophet ﷺ said, 'Fasting is a shield as long as it is not pierced'. It was asked, 'And what may pierce it?' He replied, 'Lying or backbiting.' Fasting is an impenetrable defence against torment as long as the one fasting does not breach it by lying or backbiting.

It is related on the authority of 'Ubayd ﷺ, the freed slave of Allah's Messenger ﷺ, that two women fasted and a man [who happened to be present] said, 'O Messenger of Allah, here are two women who have fasted and almost died of thirst.' He turned away from him (or remained silent); he then turned to him again and said, 'Call them.' He said, 'They have come.' He said, 'Bring a large drinking bowl,' and then he ﷺ said to one of them, 'Vomit up.' So she vomited pus, blood, purulent matter and flesh, till she filled half of the drinking bowl. Then he said to the other, 'Vomit up,' and so she vomited pus, blood, purulent matter, moist flesh and the like, till she filled the bowl. Then he ﷺ said, 'Indeed these two fasted from that which Allah has made lawful, and they broke the fast with that which Allah has made unlawful for them: one of them sat with the other and began eating from the flesh of people [i.e. backbiting them].' (Narrated by Imam Aḥmad, al-Ṭayālisī and others.)

Al-Daylamī narrated on the authority of Abū Hurayrah ﷺ, ascribing it back to the Prophet ﷺ, 'The one fasting is in [continual] worship so long as he does not backbite a Muslim or harm him.'

It, therefore, behoves the one fasting to busy himself with acts of worship, immerse himself in acts of obedience—and fervently distance himself from the sins—of the heart, limbs and tongue, especially since the month of Ramadan is the month of fasting and the season for acts of obedience and worship, when reward is multiplied and sin is magnified.

It has come in the *Ṣaḥīḥayn*, and others, that the Prophet ﷺ said, 'Whoever fasts Ramadan out of faith and in sincere anticipation of reward from Allah, Allah will forgive him his past sins; and whoever stands during the Night of the Divine Decree [in prayer] out of faith and in sincere anticipation of reward from Allah, will be forgiven his past sins.' It is related on the authority of Salmān ؓ that he said:

> The Messenger of Allah addressed us on the final day of Shaʿbān and said, 'O people, a great, blessed month has dawned on you, a month in which there is a night better than a thousand months, and a month in which Allah has made its fasting compulsory and the standing of its nights [in prayer] voluntary.
>
> Whoever draws near [to Allah] during it with an act of goodness is like the one who performs a compulsory act, and whoever performs a compulsory act during it is like the one who performs seventy compulsory acts outside of it.
>
> It is the month of patience, and the reward for patience is heaven; it is the month of charity and the month in which the sustenance (*rizq*) of a believer is increased. Whoever feeds a person who had been fasting, receives forgiveness for his sins, emancipation of his neck from hellfire, and has the like of his reward without diminishing anything from it.
>
> They said, 'O Messenger of Allah ﷺ, not all of us find something with which to feed a person who is fasting.' The Messenger of Allah ﷺ replied, 'Allah grants this reward to whoever provided a person fasting with a date to eat, a sip of water or a taste of milk.
>
> A month wherein its beginning is mercy, its middle is forgiveness and its end is emancipation from hellfire. Whoever alleviates [a burden] for his slave during it, Allah forgives him and releases him from hellfire.
>
> Increase therein in four deeds; two deeds with which you please your Lord and two you cannot do without. As for the

> two acts with which you please your Lord, they are: testifying that there is no god except Allah ("*Lā ilāha illā-Allāh*") and begging Him for forgiveness. As for the two acts which you cannot do without: asking Allah for paradise and taking refuge in Him from hellfire.
>
> Whoever gives a person who had been fasting something to drink, Allah will give him to drink from my basin—a drink by which he shall not experience thirst till he enters paradise.' (Narrated by Ibn Khuzaymah, al-Bayhaqī and others)

Al-Ṭabarānī narrated with his chain of transmission on the authority of ʿUbādah ibn al-Ṣāmit ؓ that the Messenger of Allah ﷺ said one day, 'Ramadan has come to you, a month of blessing. Allah will envelop you in it; He will cause mercy to descend, erase wrongdoings, and answer in it one's prayers. Allah Most High observes your struggle to outdo one another during it and He boasts about you to His angels, so show Allah the good from yourselves, for surely the wretched is the one who is bereft of the mercy of Allah Mighty and Majestic during it.'

Reciting the noble Qur'an profusely is sought during the month of Ramadan because it is the month in which the noble Qur'an descended in its entirety to the House of Might (*Bayt al-ʿIzzah*) in the lowest heaven. And it is the month in which it began to be revealed gradually upon the heart of the Prophet ﷺ. Therefore, to recite the noble Qur'an profusely in Ramadan has been made a sunnah, especially at night. It has been related in the *Ṣaḥīḥayn* on the authority of Ibn ʿAbbās that he said, 'The Messenger of Allah ﷺ was the most generous of people, and he was most generous in Ramadan when Jibrīl ؑ would meet him, every night of Ramadan to review the Qur'an with him. And so the Messenger of Allah ﷺ was certainly more generous with [all kinds of] good than the wind sent.'

He ﷺ would prolong the recitation of the Qur'an whilst standing in prayer during the nights of Ramadan more so than in any other month, as has been narrated by Imam Aḥmad on the authority of Ḥudhayfah ؓ, who said, 'I came to the Prophet ﷺ on one of the nights of Ramadan when he stood up to pray. When he uttered the [initial] *takbīr*,[14] he said,

الله أَكْبَرُ ذُو الْمَلَكُوتِ وَالْجَبَرُوتِ وَالْكِبْرِيَاءِ وَالْعَظَمَةِ

Allāhu akbaru dhū al-malakūti wa al-jabarūti wa al-kibriyā'i wa al-ʿaẓamah

'Allah is the greatest, possessor of sovereignty, omnipotence, grandeur and majesty.'

Then he recited al-Baqarah, al-Nisā' and then Āl ʿImrān; he would not pass by a verse that instils fear except that he paused at it."

In another narration on the authority of Ḥudhayfah ﷺ, who said, 'I prayed with the Prophet ﷺ one night. He began with al-Baqarah and recited it till he reached the end of the hundredth [verse]. So I said [to myself], "He will bow," but he proceeded to recite till he reached two hundred [verses]. So I said, "He will bow," but he proceeded to recite till he completed [the chapter]. So I said, "He will bow," but he began [reciting] al-Nisā' and he recited it [all]. Then he bowed and said in his *bowing*, "Glorified is my Lord, the Most Exalted." His bowing was like his standing (i.e. in its duration). He then prostrated, and his prostration ﷺ was like his bowing, [where] he said, "Glorified is my Lord, the Most High." When he ﷺ would come to a verse of mercy, he asked [for mercy], and when he would come to a verse of torment, he sought refuge, and when he would come to a verse that mentioned Allah Mighty and Majestic's transcendence, he glorified Him.'

ʿUmar ﷺ ordered Ubayy ibn Kaʿb and Tamīm al-Dārī ﷺ to lead the people in prayer during Ramadan. So one of them would recite two hundred [verses] in a single unit (*rakʿah*) of prayer, and they would not depart from the prayer of Ramadan (*Tarāwīḥ*) until the last portion of the night, in time to have the pre-dawn meal (*suḥūr*).

There were among the righteous early Muslim community those who would complete a recital of the entire Qur'an during the prayer of

---

14 The invocation of '*Allāhu akbar*', with which one initiates prayer.

Ramadan every three nights, those who would complete a recital every seven days and those who would complete a recital every ten days.

ʿAllāmah Ibn Ḥajar al-Haytamī said, 'Al-Shāfiʿī ﷺ would complete sixty recitals during Ramadan (i.e. a recital during the day and one during the night), which he would recite outside the prayer.' It is related about Abū Ḥanīfah ﷺ that he would do the same. When Ramadan arrived al-Zuhrī would say, 'It is nothing but reciting the Qur'an and feeding people.'

Imam Aḥmad narrated on the authority of Ibn ʿUmar ﷺ that the Messenger of Allah ﷺ said, 'Both the fast and Qur'an will intercede for the slave on the Day of Reckoning. The fast will say, "O my Lord, I deprived him of food and carnal desires during the day, and so allow me to intercede for him." The Qur'an will say, 'I deprived him of sleep throughout the night, and so allow me to intercede for him." Thus, both will intercede.'

Imam Muslim narrated on the authority of Abū Umāmah ﷺ that the Prophet ﷺ said, 'Recite the Qur'an, for it will come on the Day of Reckoning as an intercessor for its people.' The intercession of the Qur'an is only attained by one who recites it as it deserves to be recited, and that is by adhering to its injunctions: deeming lawful that which it has made lawful, and unlawful that which it has made unlawful; moulding one's character in accordance with its etiquette; and fulfilling its obligations night and day, as al-Nasāʾī narrated that when the Companion Shurayḥ al-Ḥaḍramī ﷺ was mentioned in the presence of the Prophet ﷺ, he said, 'He does not recline over the Qur'an'; meaning he does not extend sleep over it such that it becomes like a pillow for him. Rather, he fulfils the obligations of the Qur'an and its rights and is not oblivious to that.

Imam al-Nawawī mentioned regarding most of them [the early Muslims] that they would complete [a recital] every seven nights, some of them in every six nights, every five, every four; many in every three nights, some of them in every two, and some of them each day and night. Amongst them were those who would complete two recitals each day and night, those who would complete three [recitals], and some of them who would complete eight: four in the night and four in the day. This is by way of Allah Most High honouring them and making the Qur'an easy for them. He ﷺ said, 'The Recital [*Zabūr*] was made easy for Dāwūd such that he would order his mount be saddled and recite it [all] before it was saddled.'

When Ramadan would arrive, Imam al-Bukhārī would complete a recital every day during daytime, completing it by dusk each night, and would say, 'At every [complete] recital is a prayer that is answered.'

I have written in detail on this topic in my treatise *al-Adʿiyah wa al-adhkār al-wāridah ānā' al-layl wa aṭrāf al-nahār* [Transmitted supplications and invocations during the parts of the night and times of the day].

THE REQUIREMENTS AND ETIQUETTE OF FASTING

1. To profusely seek forgiveness, recite the formula 'There is no deity except Allah' ('*lā ilāha illā-Allāh*') and make much remembrance of Allah Most High. He ﷺ said, 'In Ramadan, the one who remembers Allah is forgiven, and the one who asks Allah [for some need] is not disappointed.' (Narrated by al-Ṭabarānī and others.) The words of the Prophet ﷺ have been previously mentioned, 'And increase in it four deeds: to profusely say '*lā ilāha illā-Allah*', seek forgiveness, ask for paradise and take refuge from the hellfire.'

2. To increase in giving charity in Ramadan. Al-Tirmidhī has narrated, ascribing it back to the Prophet ﷺ, 'The best [voluntary] charity is charity in Ramadan.' It has been mentioned previously in a hadith that the month of Ramadan is the month of charity, and the month in which the believer's provisions are increased. He ﷺ was most generous in Ramadan; he was not asked for anything except that he would give it, as mentioned in the narration of Imam Aḥmad.

   The month of Ramadan is a month of forgiveness, mercy, generosity and a gift from Allah Most High. Allah Most High is merciful to His merciful slaves, and the merciful are shown mercy by the Most Merciful. Whoever is generous towards the slaves of Allah Most High in this month, Allah Most High will give generously to him.

3. To take a pre-dawn meal because it is a blessed sunnah. The Two Shaykhs [al-Bukhārī and Muslim] and others narrated on the authority of Anas ibn Mālik ﵁ that the Prophet ﷺ said, 'Take the pre-dawn meal, for indeed there is blessing in it.'

   Imam Aḥmad narrated on the authority of Abū Saʿīd al-Khudrī ﵁ that the Prophet ﷺ said, 'The pre-dawn meal is a blessing, so do not miss it, even if one of you were to take a gulp of water, since Allah sends His mercy on those who take the pre-dawn meal and the angels pray for them."

   It is recommended to delay the pre-dawn meal and not to hasten in having it early due to what is [reported] in the *Musnad* from the Prophet ﷺ, who said, 'My nation will continue to be in a good state as long as they hasten to break the fast and delay the pre-dawn meal.'

4. To hasten in breaking the fast when certain of sunset. Imam Aḥmad and al-Tirmidhī narrated on the authority of Abū Hurayrah ﵁ that the Prophet ﷺ said, 'Allah Most High said, "Indeed the most beloved of My slaves to Me are the hastiest of them to break the fast."'

5. To break the fast with moist dates (*ruṭab*). If one does not find any, then with dried dates (*tamr*) and, if not, then with water. Al-Tirmidhī and others narrated on the authority of Anas ﵁ that 'The Prophet ﷺ would break the fast with moist dates before praying [*maghrib*]. If he did not find any moist dates, he would break it with dried dates, and if he did not find any dried dates, he would take sips of water'.

6. To adhere to the transmitted supplications immediately following the breaking of fast. Abū Dāwūd and others narrated on the authority of Ibn 'Umar ﵁ that he said, 'When the Prophet ﷺ would break the fast, he would say,

ذَهَبَ الظَّمَأُ، وَابْتَلَّتِ الْعُرُوقُ، وَثَبَتَ الْأَجْرُ إِنْ شَاءَ اللهُ

Dhahaba al-ẓama'u wa'b-tallati 'l-ʿuruqu wa thabata 'l-ajr in sha Allāh taʿāla

'Gone is the thirst, moistened are the veins and confirmed is the reward if Allah so wills.'

Ibn al-Sunnī narrated on the authority of Ibn ʿAbbās ﷺ that he said, 'When the Prophet ﷺ would break his fast, he would say,

اللَّهمَّ لكَ صُمتُ، وعلى رِزقِكَ أفطَرتُ فتقبَّلْ مِنِّي إنَّكَ أنتَ السَّميعُ العَليمُ.

Allāhumma laka ṣumtu wa ʿalā rizqika afṭartu fa taqabbal minnī innaka anta al-samīʿ al-ʿalīm

'O Allah, for You I have fasted and with Your sustenance I broke the fast, so accept from me. Indeed, You are the All-hearing, the All-knowing.'

In the narration of al-Dāraqūṭnī: 'When food is brought in front of one of you when he has been fasting, let him say,

بِسْمِ اللهِ وَالْحَمْدُ للهِ أللَّهُمَّ لَكَ صُمْتُ وَ عَلَى رِزْقِكَ أَفْطَرْتُ وَعَلَيْكَ تَوَكَّلْتُ سُبْحَانَكَ وَ بِحَمْدِكَ تَقَبَّلْ مِنِّي إِنَّكَ أَنْتَ السَّمِيْعُ الْعَلِيْمُ.

Bismillāhi wa al-ḥamdu li-Allāhi, Allāhumma laka ṣumtu wa ʿalā rizqika afṭartu wa ʿalayka tawakkaltu subḥānaka wa bi ḥamdika taqabbal minnī innaka anta al-samīʿ al-ʿalīm

'In the name of Allah, and all praise belongs to Allah. O Allah, forYou I have fasted, and with Your sustenance I broke the fast, and upon You I have placed my trust. Glory be to You along with Your praise; accept from me. Indeed, You are the All-hearing, the All-knowing.'

Ibn al-Sunnī narrated on the authority of Muʿādh ibn Zuhrah that he said, 'When the Prophet ﷺ would break the fast, he would say,

اَلْحَمْدُ للهِ الَّذِيْ أَعَانَنِيْ فَصُمْتُ وَ رَزَقَنِيْ فَأَفْطَرْتُ

Al-ḥamdu lillāhi lladhī aʿānanī fa ṣumtu wa razaqanī fa afṭartu

'All praise belongs to Allah, who has assisted me so I could fast, and provided me sustenance so I could break the fast.'

It is recommended that one supplicate profusely at the time of breaking the fast because it is answered. He ﷺ said, 'There are three people whose supplication is not rejected: the one fasting when he breaks fast, the just leader, and the supplication of the oppressed; Allah raises it above the clouds, the doors of the heavens are opened for it, and the Lord says, "By My might and majesty, I will most certainly come to your aid, even if it be after a while."' (Narrated by al-Tirmidhī, who graded it authentic (*ḥasan*).

ʿAbd-Allāh ibn ʿUmar ﷺ would say when breaking fast,

اللَّهُمَّ إِنِّي أَسأَلُكَ بِرَحْمَتِكَ الَّتِي وَسِعَتْ كُلَّ شَيْءٍ أَنْ تَغْفِرَلِي ذُنُوبِيْ

Allāhumma innī as'aluka bi raḥmatika llatī wasiʿat kulla shay'in an taghfira lī dhunūbī

'O Allah, I ask You by Your mercy, which encompasses everything, that You forgive me my sins.'

It behoves the one fasting to not indulge excessively in eating, nor gather various types of foods when breaking fast and having the pre-dawn meal. Rather, moderation and balance is required in all his affairs. He ﷺ said, 'It is enough for the son of Ādam to have a few morsels that keep his back upright. If he cannot do without [that], then a third for his food, a third for his drink and a third for his breath.' (Narrated by al-Tirmidhī and Ibn Mājah.)

CHAPTER THREE

The Benefits of Fasting

Fasting has many benefits of various kinds, to which our master the Messenger of Allah ﷺ has guided us, and we will mention but a few.

1. Fasting is healthy for bodies and a defence for them from illnesses, because the majority of bodily ailments are only caused by superfluity and overeating. He ﷺ said, 'Fight militarily, you shall acquire war booty; fast, you shall be healthy; and travel, you shall become wealthy.' (Narrated by al-Ṭabarānī with a chain of trustworthy narrators.)
2. Preservation of mind, rectification of thoughts, and invigoration of one's memory and minimising its forgetfulness, because gluttony increases humidity and vapours within the brain, which is something that impedes the memory.
3. Sprightliness in the movement of limbs in worship, because satiation relaxes the body and weighs it down from engaging therein. These [latter] two benefits have been indicated by his words ﷺ 'Fast, you shall be healthy.'
4. Fasting is the means to defeat Satan's aides, triumph for the troops of the All-merciful and protection for the limbs against acts of disobedience and engrossing in carnal desires, since

excessive nourishment incites the self to reprehensible desires. Therefore, when it [i.e. the self] is subjected to hunger, it is humbled, made subservient and becomes busied from having base thoughts. Thus, the limbs will be pacified from destructive acts.

When an individual fasts from wrongdoings,
Then all his months become the month of fasting.

He ﷺ said, 'Fasting is a shield'; namely, a defence against acts of disobedience, sins and the torment of the fire. And he ﷺ said, 'Fasting is a shield by which the slave guards himself from the fire.' (Narrated by Imam Aḥmad with an authenticated (*ḥasan*) chain of transmission.) Another narration, which is also his [Imam Aḥmad], has, 'Fasting is a shield and an impenetrable fortress against the fire.'

5. Fasting is the means for the fulfilment of one's hopes and the answering of one's supplications. He ﷺ said, 'Three [people] have a right upon Allah that He not reject their supplication: the one fasting up until he breaks his fast, the oppressed until he triumphs, and the traveller until he returns.'

CHAPTER FOUR
The Virtues of Fasting

Fasting has many virtues; we shall mention some of them.

1. Atonement for wrongdoings and sins. He ﷺ said, 'Whoever fasts Ramadan out of faith and anticipation [for reward], will be forgiven his past sins.' (Narrated by al-Bukhārī and others.)

   On the authority of Abū Saʿīd al-Khudrī ﷺ, the Prophet ﷺ said, 'Whoever fasts Ramadan, knows its prescriptions, and is mindful of what he ought to be mindful of, it will atone for what was before', meaning those sins that preceded the fast. (Narrated by Ibn Ḥibbān and al-Bayhaqī.)

   Muslim narrated on the authority of Abū Hurayrah ﷺ, who related that the Messenger of Allah ﷺ said, 'The five [daily] prayers, the Friday prayer to the Friday prayer, and Ramadan to Ramadan atone for what is in-between them, when major sins are avoided.'

2. Elevation of spiritual degrees and multiplication of reward. He ﷺ said, 'Every action of the son of Ādam, the good [of it] is multiplied by ten of its like, up to seven hundred. Allah Mighty and Majestic says, "Except fasting, for indeed it is for Me and I shall recompense for it: he (the one fasting) forsakes his desires and food for My sake."' (Narrated by Muslim.)

3. Fasting is a lofty station and a noble rank, and so Allah Most High ascribed it to Himself as an ennoblement. He said, 'Except fasting, for indeed it is for Me,' even though all righteous actions are for Allah Most High. This ascription, therefore, indicates a special honour. The scholars have many opinions regarding the reason for that, each of them speaking in terms of his own spiritual experience and understanding.) One proponent says: 'The one fasting finds no pleasure in fasting; thus, it is [done] for Allah alone.' Another remarks, 'Fasting is not of those actions in which ostentation may occur, because it is [mere] intention and abstinence from those things that break the fast, and so it is purely for Allah Most High, and Him alone.' There are other opinions that I have left out, for fear of misconstruction and monotony.)

4. The assembly of angels and other beings ﷺ that are with Allah find the breath from the mouth of the one fasting more pleasant than the fragrance of musk. He ﷺ said, 'By Him in whose hand is my soul, the breath from the mouth of the person fasting is more pleasant to Allah than the fragrance of musk.'

5. The angels ﷺ pray for the person fasting and seek forgiveness for him. Al-Tirmidhī and others narrated on the authority of Umm 'Ammārah al-Anṣārīyah that the Prophet ﷺ visited her outside the month of Ramadan, and she offered him food, so he said, 'Eat.' She replied, 'I am fasting.' The Messenger of Allah ﷺ said, 'Indeed, the angels pray for the one fasting when food is eaten in his presence up until they finish [eating].')

   Ibn Mājah narrated that the Prophet ﷺ said, 'O Bilāl, the bones of the one fasting glorify [Allah], and the angels seek forgiveness for him, for as long as food is eaten in his presence.'

6. Allah Mighty and Majestic boasts to the angels about those who fast. Al-Ṭabarānī narrated that the Prophet ﷺ said, 'Ramadan has come to you, a month of blessing. Allah will envelop you in it, and thus He will cause mercy to descend, erase bad deeds, answer supplications, and boast about you to His angels.')

7. Those who fast will alone enter paradise from the gate of *al-Rayyān* (the Quenched): al-Bukhārī and Muslim narrated on the authority of Abū Hurayrah that the Messenger of Allah ﷺ said, 'Whoever spends a couple [i.e. of camels or horses, or any other valuables] in Allah's path, he will be called from the gates of paradise, "O slave of Allah, this is better." And whoever was from amongst the people who prayed, will be invited from the gate of prayer, and whoever was from amongst the people of jihad [who fought for Allah's sake], will be invited from the gate of jihad, and whoever was from amongst the people who [often] fasted, will be invited from the gate of *al-Rayyān*, and whoever was amongst those who gave [a lot of] charity, will be invited from the gate of charity.' So Abū Bakr ﷺ said, 'My father and mother be your ransom, O Messenger of Allah, there is no harm for someone who is called from [all of] those gates [rather it is an honour]! So will anyone be invited from all of those gates?' He replied, 'Yes, and I hope you are from amongst them.'

8. The joy of the one fasting when breaking his fast because of securing his reward upon completing it, and his being safeguarded from anything hindering him from it, and his joy when meeting his Lord, as has been related in the *Ṣaḥīḥayn* from the Prophet ﷺ that he said, 'The one fasting takes delight in two things: in breaking his fast, and when he meets his Lord; he will rejoice because of his fasting.'

CHAPTER FIVE
The Virtues of Ramadan

INTRODUCTION

Allah Most High said: '*The month of Ramadan in which the Qur'an was revealed, as a guidance for mankind, clear signs of [His] guidance, and the criterion [between right and wrong]*' (Qur'an 2:185). There is in this evidence for the superiority of this month over the rest of the months, and its dominance over them.

Among its virtues is that in it the gates of paradise are opened and the gates of hell are closed. He ﷺ said, 'When Ramadan comes, the gates of paradise are opened, the gates of the fire closed, and the devils are shackled.' (Narrated by al-Bukhārī and Muslim.) And in a narration by Muslim, 'And the devils are chained together,' meaning fastened together with iron shackles and chains.

It has been related on the authority of Ibn Mas'ūd ؓ from the Prophet ﷺ that he said, 'When it is the first night of the month of Ramadan, the doors of paradise are opened, and so not one of its doors is closed during the entire month. And the doors of hellfire are closed, and so not one of its doors is opened during the entire month, and the rebels amongst the jinn are fettered, and a herald calls from heaven each night till the breaking of dawn, "O seeker of good, seek and rejoice, and O seeker of evil, refrain and reflect! Is there anyone who begs for forgiveness, so that we may forgive him? Is there anyone repenting whose repentance we may accept? Is there anyone supplicating, so that we may answer [his supplication]? Is there anyone imploring [Allah], so that his wish be granted?" Allah Mighty and Majestic has, at the time of breaking fast on every night of Ramadan, sixty thousand people emancipated from the fire, and when it is Eid ul-Fitr, Allah emancipates thirty times as much as those He freed during the entire month: sixty thousand, sixty thousand.' (Narrated by al-Bayhaqī, and al-Ḥāfiẓ al-Mundhirī said, 'It is a sound hadith, with no objection to it being used as a supporting narration.')

Amongst its virtues are the five qualities by which this Muhammadan nation has been distinguished, upon its Messenger be the best of blessings, peace and greetings. Imam Aḥmad, al-Bazzār and al-Bayhaqī narrated on the authority of Abū Hurayrah ﷺ that the Messenger of Allah ﷺ said, 'My nation was given five qualities in Ramadan that had never been given to any nation before it: the breath from the mouth of the one fasting is more pleasant to Allah than the fragrance of musk; fish seek forgiveness for them up until they break the fast—and in a variant narration, 'the angels seek forgiveness for them'—Allah Mighty and Majestic decks out fair His paradise every day and then says, "My upright slaves are on the brink of having their burden cast from them and coming to you (O paradise)"; and the rebellious devils are shackled, unable to do therein that which they can in other months; and they are forgiven on the last night.'

It was said, 'O Messenger of Allah, is it the Night of the Divine Decree?' He replied, 'No, rather, the one who does good deeds is given his reward in full when he completes his deed,' meaning that forgiveness is found on the last night of Ramadan.

Among its virtues is what al-Ḥākim narrated on the authority of Kaʿb ibn ʿUjrah ﷺ that he said: 'The Messenger of Allah ﷺ said, "Gather by the pulpit," so we gathered. Then when he ascended a step, he said, "Āmīn," and when he ascended the second step, he said, "Āmīn," and when he ascended the third step, he said, "Āmīn."

When he alighted, we said, "O Messenger of Allah, we heard from you today something we are not used to hearing you say?" He ﷺ replied, "Jibrīl ﵇ appeared to me (i.e. came to me) and said, 'May the one who reached Ramadan and was not forgiven be remote', so I said, "Āmīn"' (i.e. may Allah make remote he who reached the month of Ramadan, yet was neglectful in worship and repentance until the month ended and was not forgiven his sins). He ﷺ said "So when I ascended the second, Jibrīl said 'May the one who, when you are mentioned in his presence, does not send prayers upon you, be remote,' so I said "Āmīn," and when I ascended the third, Jibrīl said, "May the one whose both parents or one of them reach old age while living with him, yet they did not cause him to enter paradise, be remote" (i.e. from Allah's mercy, due to his negligence and shortcoming in fulfilling their rights), [so] I said, "Āmīn."'

THE NIGHT OF THE DIVINE DECREE (*LAYLAH AL-QADR*)

Among its virtues is that within it is the Night of the Divine Decree, which is better than a thousand months. Allah Most High said, '*We have indeed revealed it on the Night of the Divine Decree. And, what will convey to you what the Night of the Divine Decree is? The Night of the Divine Decree is better than a thousand months. The angels and the Spirit descend therein, by the permission of their Lord, with every decree. Peace, it is until the dawn break*' (Qur'an 97:1–5). In this chapter [of the Qur'an] there are numerous aspects with regard the virtue of the Night of the Divine Decree as will follow, Allah willing.

It being called the Night of the Divine Decree

It has been said that *qadr* here means rank, merit and honour, and it was named as such because it is tremendous in honour and status. One says, 'So-and-so has *qadr*', meaning honour and virtue. Or, because it confers upon the one who spends it in worship a tremendous rank, and high honour with Allah Most High. Or, because righteous deeds during it carry tremendous value and a great reward with Allah Most High, for which reason they are better than deeds [carried out] in a thousand months. And these three aspects are inseparable.

It has also been said that *qadr* here means apportionment, for it is a night in which the categorical [divine] decrees are made distinct, containing the life spans, provisions and the events of the entire world, which the angels are entrusted to execute. Allah Most High said, '*Ḥā'-Mīm.*[15] *By the Book that makes things clear. Indeed We revealed it on a blessed night, and indeed We are ever warning. When every affair of wisdom is made distinct*' (Qur'an 44:1–4), meaning it appears and issues forth from its origin, which is the *Umm al-Kitāb*,[16] as has been established from Ibn ʿAbbās ﷺ, who said regarding this verse, 'That which will happen in the year is transcribed from the *Umm al-Kitāb* on the Night of the Divine Decree, with regard provisions, life and death, or rain, to the extent that the names of those performing pilgrimage are written: "so and so will perform pilgrimage."'

The numerous virtues of this night

Firstly, it is the night on which the noble Qur'an was revealed, in which there is truth, direction and guidance for the slaves to the straightest path to felicity, supremacy, virtue, ennoblement, etiquette and high moral character. The noble Qur'an descended entirely on this night from the preserved tablet to the House of Might in the lowest heaven, and then it began to descend during this night upon our master the Messenger of Allah ﷺ, for a period of twenty-three years.

Secondly, '*The Night of the Divine Decree is better than a thousand months*' (Qur'an 97:3). What is meant by that, according to most of the early Muslims, is that a righteous deed and an act of worship on that night is better than worship in a thousand months in which

---

[15] Among the various sequences of letters revealed in the Qur'an; their meaning is unknown.

[16] Literally 'the Mother of All Books', meaning the origin of all books. It refers to the preserved tablet, wherein everything that has been pre-eternally decreed by Allah is recorded.

there is not the Night of the Divine Decree; because of that, the Prophet ﷺ urged his nation to stand in prayer during it and thus said, 'Whoever stands [in worship] during the Night of the Divine Decree, out of faith and anticipation [for reward from Allah alone], his past sins will be forgiven' (as narrated in the *Ṣaḥīḥayn*).

This is from Allah Most High's grace and His favour upon this Muhammadan nation, by virtue of its Messenger ﷺ, since He gave it a night during the year in which far-reaching stages are traversed in acts of worship, by which they attain goodness, piety, guidance and light, that no one from the previous nations attained in a thousand months without the Night of the Divine Decree, because it is better than a thousand months.

Similarly, Imam Aḥmad related from the Prophet ﷺ that he said, 'Guarding the frontier [of a Muslim land] for a day in the way of Allah is better in degrees than a thousand days [spent in something else].' Likewise, on the authority of Abū Hurayrah ؓ, the Messenger of Allah ﷺ said, 'Whoever performs six units of prayer after maghrib, not speaking ill in-between them, they [the six units] will equal the worship of twelve years.' (Narrated by al-Tirmidhī, Ibn Mājah and others.)

Imam Aḥmad narrated on the authority of ʿAbd-Allāh Ibn ʿAbbās ؓ that the Prophet ﷺ said, 'Whoever washes his hair, has a bath, draws near and reaches early [in time for the beginning of the Friday sermon], sits close and listens, has with every step he takes the [reward of] standing in prayer for a year and its [worth in] fasting.'

It is related on the authority of Aws ibn Aws al-Thaqafī ؓ that he said, 'I heard the Prophet ﷺ say, "Whoever washes his hair on Friday and has a bath, sets out and reaches early [in time for the beginning of the sermon], walks and does not ride, sits close to the imam, and then listens and does not speak in vain, has with every step the [reward of] a year's good deeds: the reward of its fasting and its standing in prayer."' (Narrated by Abū Dāwūd, al-Tirmidhī, al-Nasā'ī and others.)

Thirdly, '*The angels and the Spirit descend therein, by the permission of their Lord, with every decree*' (Qur'an 97:4). There has been disagreement over the intended meaning of the 'Spirit' here, ostensibly held to be Jibrīl ﷵ. Allah Most High said, '*With it came down the Spirit of faith and truth*' (Qur'an 6:193), and, '*Say, the Holy Spirit has brought the revelation from your Lord in truth*' (Qur'an 16:102), and He Most High said, '*Then We sent unto her Our Spirit, and it assumed for her the likeness of a perfect man*' (Qur'an 19:17). The one meant in all of this is Jibrīl ﷵ, and the Spirit (i.e. Jibrīl) is only mentioned in particular after the mention of the angels ﷵ as a mark of honour for his rank and elevated status, because he ﷺ has a unique standing. Allah Most High said in describing him, '*Endued with tremendous power, before the Lord of the Throne*' (Qur'an 81:20).

The angels and the Spirit descend during the Night of the Divine Decree and convey greetings of peace to each believer, man and woman, except the wine addict, the person persistently committing an act of disobedience, a soothsayer, or one who bears rancour. So, whosoever receives the greeting of peace (*salām*) from them, will be forgiven his past sins, as Imam al-Nawawī related from Ibn ʿAbbās ؓ.

The intended meaning of the Spirit here as Jibrīl ﷵ is further supported by what has come in the long hadith narrated by al-Bayhaqī and Ibn Ḥibbān on the authority of Ibn ʿAbbās ؓ, ascribing it back to the Prophet ﷺ: 'When it is the Night of the Divine Decree, Allah Mighty and Majestic commands Jibrīl ﷵ amongst a group of angels, who then descend and convey greetings of peace to all those standing, sitting, praying and remembering [Allah], and shake their hands, and reply "Āmīn" to their supplication till dawn break. When dawn breaks, Jibrīl ﷵ calls out, "O congregation of angels, depart, depart!" They ask, "O Jibrīl, what did Allah Most High do regarding the needs of the believers from Aḥmad's nation ﷺ?" He replies, "Allah looked upon them [out of compassion and mercy] on this night, and then pardoned and forgave them, except for four: the wine addict, the one who disrespects his parents, the one who severs the ties of kinship, and the one who bears rancour'" (i.e. the one whom rancour exists between him and his brother).[17]

So the angels and the Spirit descend during it with permission from their Lord with every matter that has been decreed for that year, or with each affair of goodness, blessing and mercy.

Fourthly, '*Peace, it is until the rising of the dawn*' (Qur'an 97:5). It is nothing but peace (i.e. greeting thereof) from the angels and the Spirit to the friends of Allah Most High, the people obedient to Him, those in mosques and every believer, man and woman, except the wine addict, the one persistent in an act of disobedience, and their like, as previously mentioned.

The angels greet the believers, men and women, and convey to them the greeting of peace from their Lord, Most Blessed and High, as has been related from the early pious Muslim community. This is why tranquillity and security descends and envelops the believers, which lasts till the breaking of dawn.

One of the exacting scholars among the gnostics has said: 'The Night of the Divine Decree is applicable to two nights. The first, meaning rank and merit, and that is what Allah Most High described with His words "*The Night of tbe Divine Decree is better than a thousand months*", and this is exclusively in the last ten [days] of Ramadan. The second, with the meaning of apportionment, and that is what Allah Most High described with His words "*Indeed, We revealed it on a blessed night, and indeed We are ever warning. In it is made distinct every affair of wisdom*" (Qur'an 44:3–4), and this night rotates throughout the entire year, though usually it is the night of mid-Shaʿbān. The two nights coincided on the night in which the noble Qur'an descended; therefore, it was described with both qualities, namely, with rank and merit, and with apportionment and distinction.' This opinion is the final word on this issue because it includes the variant positions.

---

[17] See *al-Targhīb wa al-tarhīb* by al-Ḥāfiẓ al-Mundhirī, who said, 'There is not in the chain of narration of this hadith any narrator who is considered unanimously weak.'

Standing in worship on the Night of the Divine Decree

It has been related on the authority of Abū Hurayrah ﵁ that the Messenger of Allah ﷺ said, 'Whoever stands [in prayer] during the Night of the Divine Decree, out of faith and anticipation [for reward], will be forgiven his past sins.' (Agreed upon [by al-Bukhārī and Muslim])

Imam al-Nawawī said, 'The meaning of standing therein in worship 'out of faith' is believing it to be true and an act of obedience, and 'anticipation' is seeking the pleasure of Allah Most High and His reward, and not out of ostentation and the like.'

It is therefore sunnah to profusely pray, supplicate and perform other acts of worship during it, and it is recommended to spend it awake in worship. It should be sought in the final ten [days] of Ramadan due to what al-Bukhārī narrated on the authority of Lady ʿĀ'ishah that the Messenger of Allah ﷺ said, 'Pursue the Night of the Divine Decree in the last ten [days] of Ramadan.'

It is related in the *Ṣaḥīḥayn* that when the final ten days would arrive, the Prophet ﷺ would spend the night in worship, wake his family, and strive and exert himself in worship.

Its reward is attained by whoever stands therein in prayer, corresponding to it, even if none of its lights and special qualities were disclosed to him, whether in wakefulness or in a dream, due to what has come in the narration of Muslim, that the Prophet ﷺ said, 'Whoever stands in prayer during the Night of the Divine Decree, thus coinciding with it, out of faith and anticipation, will be forgiven for his past sins.'

It is recommended that one profusely supplicates during that night with the supplication transmitted from Lady ʿĀ'ishah that she said, 'I said, "Tell me, O Messenger of Allah, if I know that it is the Night of the Divine Decree, what should I say during it?" He replied, "Say,

اللَّهُمَّ إِنَّكَ عَفُوٌّ تُحِبُّ الْعَفْوَ فَاعْفُ عَنِّي.

Allāhumma innaka ʿafuwwun karīmun tuḥibbu l-ʿafwa faʿfu ʿannī

'O Allah, indeed You are oft-pardoning, generous, You love to pardon, so pardon me.'

Al-Tirmidhī graded it a rigorously authenticated narration (*ṣaḥīḥ*).

The signs of the Night of the Divine Decree

The sun rises as if white on the [following] morning, without any visible rays, due to the bright strength of the lights descending during its night, the vast number of angels descending, and the tranquillity and subtle spiritual things spreading between the heavens and earth that descend with them.

It has come in the *Ṣaḥīḥ* of Muslim on the authority of Ubayy ibn Kaʿb ؓ that he said, 'By Him besides whom there is no god, it [the Night of the Divine Decree] is in Ramadan. And it is the night during which the Messenger of Allah ﷺ ordered us to stand in prayer. And it is the twenty-seventh night. And its sign is that the sun rises in its morning, white without any rays.'

It is related in the *Musnad* of Imam Aḥmad with a good chain of narration, on the authority of 'Ubādah ibn al-Ṣāmit ؓ, that the Messenger of Allah ﷺ said, 'The sign of the Night of the Divine Decree is that it is serene and clear, as though a radiant moon is in it, still and tranquil, neither cold nor hot, and no shooting star is permitted therein till dawn breaks; and that the sun in its morning emerges level, without a ray, like a full moon, and on that day it is not permitted for Satan to emerge with it [i.e. the sun].'

The signs found on the Night of the Divine Decree increase the believer's vigour and motivate him to stand in prayer and worship during it. The sign in its morning encourages one to increase in worship on its following day, since the light of the Night of the Divine Decree and its blessings extend to its following day, which is why Imam al-Nawawī cites in *al-Majmūʿ*, 'It is recommended (*mustaḥabb*) that a believer exert himself in worship on the following day, just as he did during the Night of the Divine Decree.'

THE PRAYER OF TARĀWĪḤ: ITS PROOF AND MERIT

It is related in the *Ṣaḥīḥayn* on the authority of Abū Hurayrah ﷺ that the Messenger of Allah ﷺ said, 'Whoever stands in prayer in Ramadan out of faith and anticipation will be forgiven his past sins.'

Al-Nasā'ī narrated that the Prophet ﷺ said, 'Whoever stands in prayer in Ramadan out of faith and anticipation will part from his sins like the day his mother gave birth to him.' In another narration of his, the Prophet ﷺ said, 'Allah has made the fasting of Ramadan obligatory (*farḍ*), and I have made its standing in prayer a sunnah for you; therefore, whoever fasted in it and stood in it in prayer, out of faith and anticipation, will part from his sins like the day his mother gave birth to him.' What is meant by standing in prayer in Ramadan is the prayer of *Tarāwīḥ*.

Its ruling and number

The prayer of *Tarāwīḥ* is an emphasised sunnah (*sunnah mu'akkadah*) for men and women, and its performance in congregation is a communal sunnah (*sunnah 'alā al-kifāyah*). It is twenty cycles of prayer as has been established by proofs, and upon which the masses of the Imams have concurred. We have mentioned a summary of the proofs of it being twenty cycles in our treatise *al-Ad'iyah wa al-adhkār*, so refer to it there.

ṢADAQAH AL-FIṬR: ITS PROOF AND MERIT

It is related on the authority of Ibn 'Abbās ﷺ that he said, 'The Messenger of Allah ﷺ made *ṣadaqah al-fiṭr* obligatory (*farḍ*) as a purification for the one fasting from vain and vulgar talk, and as a food for the deprived. So whoever discharged it before the [Eid] prayer, then it is an accepted zakat, and whoever discharged it after the prayer, then it is a voluntary charity.' (Narrated by Abū Dāwūd)

Its ruling and amount

It is necessary (*wājib*) according to Imams Abū Ḥanīfah and al-Shāfiʿī, and its amount is two kilograms of wheat for each individual. It is permissible to give its [monetary] value according to the Hanafī school.

THE EID UL-FITR PRAYER: ITS PROOF AND MERIT

It is related in the *Ṣaḥīḥayn*, on the authority of Ibn ʿAbbās ﵄, that the Messenger of Allah ﷺ came out on Eid ul-Fitr and prayed two cycles. He did not pray [any cycles] before or after them.

With his chain of transmission, al-Ṭabarānī narrated from the Prophet ﷺ that he said, 'When it is the day of Eid ul-Fitr, the angels stop at the gates of roads and call, "Come early, O congregation of Muslims, to a Most Generous Lord, who will bestow graciously with good and then reward you abundantly for it. Surely, you have been commanded to stand the night in prayer, so you stood, and you were commanded to fast during the day, so you fasted and obeyed your Lord, so take a hold of your rewards." So when they pray, a herald announces, "Surely, your Lord has forgiven you, so return, guided to your mounts." It is the "Day of the Award", and thus is it named in the heavens.'

Its ruling and an explanation of the additional takbīrs

The Eid prayer is necessary (*wājib*) according to Imam Abū Ḥanīfah and sunnah according to Imam al-Shāfiʿī. It is two cycles of prayer with six additional *takbīr*s according to the Hanafī school: three in the first cycle after the extolment (*thanā*) and three in the second after the recitation before bowing. According to the Shāfiʿī school, there are seven *takbīr*s in the first cycle before the recitation, and five *takbīr*s in the second cycle also before the recitation.

FASTING SIX DAYS OF SHAWWĀL

It is recommended for a Muslim to fast six days from the month of Shawwāl unconditionally, even if he does not do so immediately after Eid ul-Fitr. The Messenger of Allah ﷺ said, 'Whoever fasts Ramadan and then follows it with six [days] of Shawwāl, it will be like fasting a lifetime.' (Narrated by Muslim.)

May Allah bless and send salutations upon our master Muhammad, his family and Companions. '*Glorified be your Lord, the Lord of Majesty! [He is free] from what they ascribe [to Him]. And peace be upon the messengers. And all praise be to Allah, the Lord of the Worlds*' (Qur'an 37:180—2).

This treatise was completed on the 1st of Ramadan 1384 H, and all praise be to Allah, the Lord of the Worlds.

Treatise Two

Al-Ṣawm

SHAYKH MUḤAMMAD HISHĀM BURHĀNĪ

بسم الله الرحمن الرحيم

AUTHOR'S INTRODUCTION TO THE FIRST EDITION

All praise belongs to Allah, the Lord of the Worlds. May His blessings and peace be upon His messenger, the noblest of all creation, and upon the pure members of his household, and his Companions who raised the banner of truth and guidance, East and West, and those who follow them and are guided by their guidance, until the Day of Reckoning.

To proceed: the splendid reverberation with which the epistle ('Prayer')[18] was received and clearly manifested by people's interest in it with fascination and enthusiasm, and its widespread distribution, not in Syria alone, but rather in other Arab countries also, and some Muslim minorities in foreign countries, compelled us to publish it once, twice, and a third time ... all of which was through Allah Most High's grace (*tawfiq*).

This is why, with the pressing need which has arisen due to people's disregard to studying the books of Islamic jurisprudence and their not attending the gatherings of knowledge, we made a firm resolve, relying upon Allah Mighty and Majestic, to contribute in filling this void, and so we present to our believing brethren successive epistles

---

[18] This epistle has been translated into English and published by Heritage Press under the title '*A Believer's Guide to Prayer*'.

which provide them essential Islamic jurisprudential education, so that no excuse remains for the in-different, nor any justification for the negligent.

We presented, while recognising our shortcomings, what we intended to publish before having it printed, to the eminent teachers Shaykh ʿAbd al-Wahhab 'Dibs wa Zayt' and Shaykh Muḥammad Saʿīd Burhānī for them to offer their insights before these epistles reach the hands of the readers, so that our steps may be more conducive to instilling confidence and peace of mind.

Therefore, we present this epistle ('Fasting') of ours to every believer, hoping that the Generous Master will accept it from us, so that His servants may benefit from it.

- MUḤAMMAD HISHĀM BURHĀNĪ

NOBLE VERSES FROM THE QUR'AN

1. O you who believe, fasting has been prescribed for you, as it was prescribed for those before you, that you may become God-conscious [by guarding yourself from those things which incur His displeasure].

2. [That is] for a specified number of days; and whoever amongst you is ill, or on a journey, [such that he does not fast, he is then obliged to fast] a number of other days [after Ramadan to make up those days he did not fast in Ramadan]. And for those who are able [to fast but do not] the *fidyah*[19] is incumbent upon them, which is feeding a poor man, but whosoever voluntarily gives good [more than the required amount of *fidyah*], then it is better for him; and for you to fast would be better for you, if you only knew.

3. The month of Ramadan in which the Qur'an was revealed, as a guidance for mankind, clear signs of [His] guidance, and the criterion [between right and wrong]. And whoever amongst you witnesses [the new moon], then let him fast the month, and whosoever of you is sick or on a journey, then [let him fast] an equal number of other days. Allah desires for you ease and He desires not

---

[19] Literally, the ransom, which is the substitute given to a poor person, equivalent to two kilograms of whole-wheat flour.

hardship for you; and [He desires that] you complete the prescribed period, and to glorify Him in that which He has guided you; and perchance you shall be grateful.

4. It is made lawful for you to go unto your wives on the night of the fast. They are raiment for you and you are raiment for them. Allah is aware that you were deceiving yourselves in this respect and He has turned in mercy toward you and relieved you, so approach them now and seek what Allah has ordained for you, and eat and drink until the white thread of dawn appears to you distinct from its black thread; then complete your fast till the night appears; but do not associate with your wives while you are in retreat in the mosques. Those are the limits imposed by Allah, so approach them not. Thus Allah makes clear His signs to mankind, that they may become God-conscious. (Qur'an 2:183–5; 187)

NOBLE HADITHS

1. When Ramadan comes, the gates of paradise are opened, and the gates of hellfire are closed.
2. Fasting is half of patience, and patience is half of faith.
3. O congregation of youth, whoever among you is able to marry should do so, for it is most effective in lowering the gaze [from the unlawful] and preserving one's chastity, and whoever is unable, then he should fast, for indeed it is a protection for him.
4. Whoever does not abstain from false accusation and acting in accordance with it, then Allah is in no need of his abstaining from food and drink.
5. Allah Mighty and Majestic said: 'Every deed of the son of Ādam is for him except fasting, for indeed that is for Me and I will recompense him for it. And fasting is a guard, so when it is one of the days that you fast, then let him not speak obscenely, nor yell; if anyone abuses him or fights him, let him say, "I am fasting, I am fasting." By Him in whose hand is Muhammad's soul ﷺ, the breath from the mouth of the one fasting is more pleasant to Allah than the fragrance of musk. The one fasting is joyous of two delights: when he breaks his fast, he is joyous of breaking

his fast, and when he meets his Lord, he is joyous of his fast [i.e. of its reward].' (Narrated by al-Bukhārī and Muslim.)

6. Verily, there is in Paradise a door called *al-Rayyān* ['the Quenched']. Those who fast enter through it on the Day of Resurrection, and none besides. Once they have entered, it will be closed and no one else shall enter through it. (Narrated by al-Bukhārī and Muslim.)
7. Fasting is a guard and fortified fortress against the fire. (Narrated by Aḥmad and al-Bayhaqī.)
8. The fast and the Qur'an will intercede for the servant on the Day of Resurrection: the fast shall say, 'My Lord, I deprived him of food and carnal desire, so permit me to intercede for him,' and the Qur'an will say, 'I deprived him of sleep at night, so permit me to intercede for him.' He ﷺ said, 'So they will be permitted to intercede.' (Narrated by Aḥmad, al-Ṭabarānī and others.)
9. There is not a servant who fasts a day for the sake of Allah except that Allah distances his face from the hellfire by seventy years [lit, seventy autumns] because of that day. (Narrated by al-Bukhārī and Muslim.)
10. There are three people whose prayer is not rejected: the one fasting when he breaks his fast, the upright leader and the prayer of the oppressed. Allah raises it above the clouds, the gates of heaven are opened for it and the Lord says, 'By My might and majesty, I shall most certainly come to your aid, even if it be after a while.' (Narrated by Aḥmad and al-Tirmidhī.)
11. Whosoever fasts Ramadan, out of faith and anticipation [of reward from Allah], will be forgiven his previous sins. (Narrated by al-Bukhārī and Muslim.)
12. It has been related from Ka'b ibn 'Ujrah that he said: 'The Messenger of Allah ﷺ said, "Gather at the pulpit," and so we did. When he ﷺ climbed a step, he said, "Āmīn," and when he went up the second step, he said, "Āmīn," and when he went up the third, he said, "Āmīn." When he descended, we said, "O Messenger

of Allah, we heard from you today something which we are not accustomed to." He ﷺ replied, "Indeed, Jibrīl (upon whom be peace) appeared before me and said, 'The one who reaches Ramadan and is not forgiven, may he be remote [from the mercy of Allah].' I said 'Āmīn'; then when I went up the second, and he said, 'The one who does not invoke blessings on you when you are mentioned, may he be remote,' so I said 'Āmīn'; and when I went up the third, he said, 'The one whose both parents or one of them reach old age in his lifetime and are not a cause for him to enter paradise [while they are with him], may he be remote,' so I said "Āmīn." (Narrated by al-Ḥākim.)

13. Whoever invalidates a day's fast in Ramadan without a dispensation or illness, fasting an entire lifetime would not compensate for it, even if he were to fast it (in terms of reward, not its obligation being lifted).

CHAPTER ONE

Preliminaries of Fasting Ramadan

RECEIVING RAMADAN

Muslims should receive the month of fasting with repentance, sincerity and vigour in worship. It has been related that the Messenger a used to give glad tidings to his Companions and say, 'The month of Ramadan has come to you, a blessed month. Allah has made mandatory its fast and during it, the gates of heaven are opened, the gates of hellfire are closed, and the devils are shackled; in it is a night that is better than a thousand months, and the one who is deprived of its goodness is truly deprived.' Consequently, the righteous early Muslim community (*al-salaf al-ṣāliḥ*) used to welcome and rejoice at its arrival more fervently than rejoicing at the arrival of their absent ones, in emulation of him ﷺ, for he used to supplicate when the month of Rajab would begin with his words,

اللَّهُمَّ بَارِكْ لَنَا فِي رَجَبٍ، وَشَعْبَانَ، وَبَلِّغْنَا رَمَضَانَ.

Allāhumma bārik lanā fī rajaba wa shaʿbāna wa ballighnā ramaḍān

'O Allah, bless us in Rajab and Shaʿbān and enable us to reach Ramadan.'

In the beginning of Islam, fasting used to be for three days of every Arab month and the day of *'Āshūrā'* [The tenth of Muḥarram]. Later, it was abrogated by the obligation to fast Ramadan in the second year of the Hejira before the Battle of Badr. Fasting was not, in the beginning of its obligation, in the form that we know it today, but rather developed, as has been related in the hadith, 'They used to eat, drink and copulate with their wives as long as they did not fall asleep, and when they fell asleep, they would be obliged to abstain from food, drink and copulation. Then [one day] a man from the Medinan Helpers (*Anṣār*), named Ṣurmah, after praying *'ishā'* fell asleep, [as] he was suffering from fatigue. After a while, his wife woke him up, and as he was not one to disobey Allah and His Messenger, he refused to eat and awoke in the morning fasting and exhausted. It had not reached midday when he had fainted. When he regained consciousness, he came to the Prophet ﷺ, who upon seeing him, said, "O Abū al-Qays, why did you spend the evening feeble and exhausted?" When he mentioned to him ﷺ his condition, the Messenger of Allah ﷺ became distressed.' It so happened that 'Umar ؓ had intercourse with one of his wives after he had slept, so he came to the Prophet ﷺ and mentioned that to him, whereupon, Allah Most High revealed, '*It is made lawful for you to go unto your wives on the night of the fast ...*' up to His words '*then complete your fast till the night appears*.'

SEEKING THE NEW MOON OF RAMADAN

It is obligatory for any given community of Muslims to look for the new moon of Ramadan on the evening of the twentyninth of Sha'bān at sunset, and it is necessary for whoever sees it to go and inform the qadi of that. If he does not go, or he goes but the judge rejects his statement, it is necessary for him to fast the following morning because of the Most High's words, '*Whoever from amongst you witnesses the month, then let him fast it*.' As for someone who alone sees the new moon of Shawwāl and whose statement is rejected, then it is necessary for him to fast and unlawful for him not to, because of his saying ﷺ, 'Your non-observance of fasting is the day you collectively abstain.' And since the people have not ceased fasting, it is obligatory for him to continue too.

Ramadan is established by the sighting of its new moon, or Shaʿbān's completion of thirty days if the new moon is obstructed [from view] by fog or something else, because of his saying a, 'Fast upon sighting it, and cease fasting upon sighting it. And if it is obstructed from you, then complete the number of days of Shaʿbān as thirty.' If there is an obstruction in the sky, the testimony of an adult Muslim who is sane, upright (uprightness being the faculty that induces one to adhere to God-consciousness (*taqwā*) and social integrity (*murūʾah*)) or a *mastūr* (someone who neither his uprightness nor immorality is evident) is sufficient for the establishment of Ramadan. If the sky is clear, the sighting of a group is necessary for its establishment.

As for the new moon of *fiṭr* [Shawwāl], if there is obstruction in the sky, then the testimony of two free [not enslaved] legally responsible (*mukallaf*)[20] males, or a male and two female, Muslims is necessary. If the sky is clear, then the sighting [of the new moon] by a group is necessary. No consideration is given to the opinion of astronomers with regards to the obligation to fast or to cease fasting, so their statement that 'The moon shall be born on suchand-such night' is disregarded. Moreover, it is impermissible for the astronomer himself to act upon his own calculation, because the obligation to fast or to cease fasting is dependent on visual sighting, due to his words a 'Fast upon sighting it'.

It is sought from whoever sees the new moon to say, 'O Allah, make it dawn upon us with security, faith, protection, submission and the ability to do that which pleases You. My Lord and your Lord is Allah,' as has been related from him ﷺ.

There is no consideration given to the variant points of the moon's ascent; if the sighting of the new moon is established in any [one] of the Muslim regions, it becomes incumbent upon all

---

20 An individual who has reached puberty and is sane.

people of all regions [to follow] if it is established amongst them by a channel that makes it binding [upon them to fast], such as two people bearing testimony or the news becoming widespread. Therefore, if Ramadan is established, for instance, in Egypt, a day before us, it is necessary for us to make up the fast of that day.

It is offensive to fast the 'Day of Doubt', which is the day that follows the twenty-ninth of Shaʿbān, when both knowledge and the lack thereof, regarding the reality of the situation, are equal.[21] It is not offensive, however, to fast during it with the sole intention of a voluntary fast. Whoever wakes up in the morning fasting on the 'Day of Doubt' with the intention of a voluntary fast or another fast, and it subsequently becomes apparent that this day was Ramadan, his fast will be considered that of Ramadan, since it is a time allotted solely and specifically for a single act of worship (*miʿyār*) that cannot accommodate another [fast].

---

[21] Namely, it is equally possible for it to be the thirtieth of Shaʿbān or the first of Ramadan.

CHAPTER TWO

The Significance, Definition, Prerequisites and Types of Fasting

ITS SIGNIFICANCE IN ISLAM

Fasting is one of the five pillars of Islam, and whosoever denies and rejects it is deemed a disbeliever, while whoever neglects it is deemed legally immoral (*fāsiq*).

ITS DEFINITION

It is the abstinence from those things that would otherwise break it, whether deliberately (*'amd*) or unintentionally (*khaṭa'*), from dawn to dusk, accompanied by an intention to fast. The *'āmid*[22] is someone who intends to take something which breaks the fast. The *mukhṭi'*[23] (unintentional) is like someone who while gargling during wuḍū', for instance, water spontaneously enters his body cavity. If this occurs during [a fast] outside of Ramadan, it is necessary for him to only make up the fast of that day without refraining from eating and drinking during that day. If, however, it was during Ramadan, it would be necessary for him to refrain [from eating and drinking]

[22] Literally, one who does an act deliberately.

[23] Literally, one who does an act mistakenly or unintentionally.

for the remainder of that day, out of reverence for the month, and make up that day.

THE CONDITIONS FOR ITS OBLIGATION

1. Islam: A non-Muslim is not required to fast, nor is it valid from other than a Muslim.
2. Puberty and sanity: It is not obligatory upon an insane person, or a child who has not reached puberty; however, someone who reaches seven years of age is ordered to fast, so that he may become accustomed to it. If he fasts, it would be valid from him and both he and his parents are rewarded.
3. Good health: is a condition for the obligation to observe it [within the month], due to the Most High's saying, '*And whosoever of you witnesses [the new moon], let him fast the month, and whosoever of you is sick or on a journey, then [let him fast] an equal number of other days*.' So if he were to burden himself and fast, it would still be valid.
4. Absence of menses and lochia: thus it is not valid from a woman during menses or lochia; rather, it is necessary for her to abstain from fasting and to make it up later. Likewise, the absence of anything that nullifies the fast is a condition [for its validity, not its obligation], as long as the one who takes it [something that nullifies it, such as food or drink] does not do so absent-mindedly.
5. Absence of major ritual impurity:[24] is not conditional for its validity; hence, if he was subject to it [major ritual impurity] during the night, and woke up in such a state, his fast would be valid, though he would have to wash himself for the prayer.

---

[24] This is a state of ritual impurity caused by intercourse or a woman's release of menstrual fluid or lochia. The state necessitates a purificatory bath (*ghusl*) to lift one out of that state. In this state prayer, whether performed after ablution or not, mere recitation of the Qur'an and entering a mosque are all prohibited.

Similar to him is someone who sleeps during the day in Ramadan and has a wet dream; his fast is not nullified, though he washes himself for the prayer (its explanation is to follow).

6. Residence: Hence, it is not necessary for a traveller[25] to fast in Ramadan during his journey. Instead, he makes it up afterwards, although it would be better for him to fast during the journey if it did not pose any hardship for him or if most of his travelling companions were fasting, because of the Most High's words '*and for you to fast, is better for you*'.
7. Intention (for each day): so that an act of worship may be distinguished from a mere habitual practice [of fasting, in this case], and it will be expounded upon later if Allah so wills.

ITS RULING

In this world, to discharge one's obligation if the fast was necessary (*wājib*) and compulsory (*lāzim*), whether obligatory (*farḍ*) or otherwise. In the afterlife, it is reward, out of Allah Most High's generosity.

ITS CATEGORIES

1. Personally obligatory (*farḍ al-ʿayn*),[26] which is the fast of Ramadan (within its time), the making up of such a fast (when he makes up that for which he is accountable), and the fast of the various atonements (such as the atonement for *ẓihār*,[27] deliberate

---

[25] One becomes a traveller, once one leaves the borders of his home-city and intends to travel 50 miles (81km) according to some scholars, while according to others 57 miles (95km) or more from there, and the traveller becomes a resident once again if he returns home or intends residence at a location for fifteen days or more.

[26] An act that is compulsory, for each Muslim to perform individually. The term *farḍ* refers to a firm command based upon decisive textual evidence, either from the Qur'an or mass-transmitted narration (*mutawātir hadīth*), whose meaning is explicit and not subject to interpretation. One must believe in and act upon a *farḍ*: disbelief is feared for the one who denies it, and the one who fails to act upon it is sinful.

[27] A practice from the pre-Islamic times of ignorance: when a man would become angry with his wife and did not want her to marry someone else, he would say to

breaking of a fast in Ramadan, the atonement for manslaughter or for breaking an oath).

2. Necessary (*wājib*):[28]

a) Making up of voluntary fasts that one has nullified, and similarly, completing a voluntary fast once one has commenced it;

b) The fast during *iʿtikāf*[29] (the spiritual retreat) that one has vowed to perform; thus whoever vows to perform *iʿtikāf* for ten days, for instance, it becomes necessary for him to fast during those days while he is in his place of *iʿtikāf*.

3. Sunnah:[30] the fast of *ʿĀshūrāʾ*, together with the fast of the ninth or eleventh [of Muḥarram], because of his fasting ﷺ the tenth and his words ﷺ 'If I remain till the coming year, I shall fast the ninth.' The Messenger ﷺ was asked about fasting the day of *ʿĀshūrāʾ*, to which he replied, 'It atones for [the sins of] the previous year.' It has been related from Ibn ʿAbbās ﷺ, 'The Messenger of Allah fasted the day of *ʿĀshūrāʾ* and ordered that it be fasted.' (Narrated by al-Bukhārī and Muslim.)

---

her, 'You are like my mother's back.' Consequently, she would become forever unlawful for him and remain suspended—neither married nor divorced. Islam abolished this practice and strongly deters against it by imposing an expiation upon anyone who does it. Legally speaking, it is a man's comparing his wife to a woman, or her limb, unlawful for him to look at, who is permanently unmarriageable kin, like his mother or sister.

[28] A firm command based upon textual evidence that is subject to interpretation. The one who denies something that is *wājib* is deemed a *fāsiq*, and the one who fails to act upon it is a degree less sinful than someone who fails to act upon a *farḍ*.

[29] Staying in a mosque, usually for the final ten days of Ramadan, where the five daily prayers are performed in congregation. A woman performs *iʿtikāf* in the part of the home that has been designated for prayer (i.e. the area in which she habitually prays).

[30] Also known as *sunnah muʾakkadah* or an emphasised sunnah: an action that was regularly performed by the Prophet ﷺ and his Companions. Leaving it is considered blameworthy but not sinful, though it is sinful to leave it habitually.

4. Recommended (*mandūb*):[31]

a) Fasting three days every month, and it is recommended that they are the white days, which are the thirteenth, fourteenth and fifteenth [of the lunar month].

It has been related from Abū Hurayrah ﵁ that he said, 'My intimate friend [i.e. the Messenger of Allah] ﷺ exhorted me to do three things: fasting three days of every month, the two units of *ḍuḥā*[32] and the *witr*[33] prayer before going to sleep.' (Narrated by al-Bukhārī, Muslim and al-Nasā'ī.)

He ﷺ said, 'Fasting three days every month is [equivalent to] fasting one's entire lifetime.' (Narrated by al-Bukhārī and Muslim.)

It has been related from 'Abd-Allāh ibn 'Amr ibn al-'Āṣ ﵄ that the Prophet ﷺ said to him, 'I have been told that you fast during the day and stand during the night [in prayer]. Do not do so, since your body has a right over you, your eyes have a share over you and your wife has a share over you. Fast and break the fast; fast three days of every month, for that is the fast of a lifetime.' He said, 'O Messenger of Allah, I have the ability.' He replied, 'Then observe the fast of Dāwūd ﵇: fast a day and do not fast the next [day].' So he ['Abd-Allāh ibn 'Amr] used to say, 'If only I had taken the dispensation.' (Narrated by al-Bukhārī and Muslim.)

b) Fasting Mondays and Thursdays: It has been related from Abū Hurayrah ﵁ that the Prophet ﷺ used to fast Mondays and Thursdays, so he was asked, 'O Messenger of Allah, [why do] you fast Mondays and Thursdays?' He ﷺ replied, 'Verily, on Mondays and Thursdays Allah forgives every Muslim except

---

[31] An act that was occasionally performed by the Prophet ﷺ: its performance is rewarded, while its omission does not entail sin nor blame.

[32] The mid-morning prayer: a non-compulsory sunnah prayer that is performed after the sun has fully risen and prior to its reaching its zenith.

[33] Literally, the 'odd-numbered prayer': three units of prayer (necessary according to the Ḥanafī school) performed after the *'ishā'* prayer.

two people who shun one another, saying, "Leave them until they reconcile between themselves."' (Narrated by Ibn Mājah.)

c) Fasting six days of Shawwāl: The Messenger of Allah ﷺ said, 'Whoever fasts Ramadan and then follows it up with six [days of fasting] from Shawwāl, it will be as if fasting an entire lifetime.' (Narrated by Muslim, al-Tirmidhī and Abū Dāwūd.)

d) The fast of the 'month of Allah', Muḥarram: The Messenger of Allah ﷺ said, 'The best fast after Ramadan is the fast of Allah's month Muḥarram and the best prayer after the obligatory prayer is the prayer during the night.'

e) Fasting in Shaʿbān: it has been related from ʿĀ'ishah that she said, 'The Messenger of Allah used to fast to the extent that we would say, "He does not break fast." And he would abstain from fasting to the extent that we would say, He does not fast," and I have never seen him fast an entire month except Ramadan, and I have not seen him fast in a month [other than Ramadan] more sthan Shaʿbān.' (Narrated by al-Bukhārī, Muslim and others.)

5. A voluntary fast is anything besides the aforementioned: those fasts that have not been established by the Lawgiver to contain any offence, nor has a time been specified for them.

6. The offensive fast is of two types:

a) Slightly offensive:[34]

i) like the fast of *ʿĀshūrā'* in isolation from the ninth or eleventh of Muḥarram;

ii) fasting Friday alone due to his words ﷺ 'Do not distinguish Friday night from other nights by standing [in prayer] and do not distinguish Friday from other days by fasting unless it is a fast that one of you normally observes'; namely, by fasting a day before or after it;

---

[34] *Makrūh tanzīhī*: an act whose avoidance has been recommended and is rewarded; its performance is blameworthy, though no sin is entailed.

iii) fasting Saturday alone because of his words ﷺ 'Do not fast Saturday unless it is a day that has been made obligatory for you. If one of you does not find anything except the skin of a grape or a twig of a tree, then let him chew it';

iv) fasting the first day of spring (*nayrūz*) or autumn (*mahrajān*) alone, for these two days were Persian festivals. If they coincide with one's habitual fast, there is no offence in fasting them.

b) Severely offensive:[35]

i) fasting the first day of the two Eids;

ii) fasting the days of *Tashrīq*: the second, third and fourth day of Eid ul-Adha;

iii) the fast of continuity (*al-wiṣāl*), which is fasting two or three entire days consecutively without drinking or eating between them, as it is offensive for other than the Prophet ﷺ;

iv) the perpetual fast: if it debilitates one from one's obligations and necessarily earning a living, then it is severely offensive, otherwise it is slightly offensive as it becomes a mere habit, while the basis of worship is for it to be contrary to that which is merely habitual.

Imam Muslim narrated one of the Companions saying, 'I used to fast continuously and read the Qur'an every night, so either I mentioned [this] to the Prophet ﷺ, or he called for me and I went, and he ﷺ said, "Have I not been informed that you fast perpetually and read the Qur'an every night?" I replied, "Certainly, O Prophet of Allah, and I only intended good thereby." He said, "It is sufficient for you to fast three days of every month." I replied, "I am able to do better than that." He replied, "Indeed your wife has a right over you, your visitor has a right over you and your body has a right over you, so observe the fast of Dāwūd عليه السلام, for indeed he was the

35 *Makrūh taḥrīmī*: an act whose avoidance has been emphatically commanded with textual proof that is subject to interpretation; performing such an action is deemed sinful.

most devout of people." I asked, "O Prophet of Allah, what is the fast of Dāwūd?" He replied, "He would fast a day and not fast the next'":

v) a woman's observing a voluntary fast without the [prior] permission of her husband. He has the right to have her break it so that she may fulfil his rights and see to his needs, except when it entails him no harm. If he has her break the fast, it becomes necessary for her to make it up. As for the obligatory fast, like making up a fast of Ramadan, for instance, then it is not dependent upon his consent, because neglecting it is considered disobedience [to Allah]; there is no obedience to creation when it entails disobedience to the Creator. He ﷺ said, 'It is not permissible for a woman to fast when her husband is present except with his permission, or to allow someone in his house except with his permission, or to give charity from his wealth.' What is meant from the hadith is a voluntary fast. (Narrated by al-Bukhārī and Muslim.)

THE INTENTION

A fast, whether obligatory, necessary or voluntary, within its time or made up afterwards, must be accompanied by an intention. The timing of this intention differs according to the type of fast observed.

Firstly, there is a category in which it is neither conditional to intend from the night, nor to specify it [i.e. the intention] for the fast one is observing:

1. a fast of Ramadan [during the month];
2. a vow in which the time is specified, such as one's saying, 'I hereby owe Allah the fast of this Thursday'; an unconditional voluntary fast, meaning one that is not obligatory, necessary or recommended.
3. an unconditional voluntary fast, meaning one that is not obligatory, necessary or recommended.

Regarding these three types of fast, they are valid even if the one fasting does not intend from the night since it is permissible for him to intend once the day has begun until approximately fifty minutes before *ẓuhr*. Neither is it conditional to specify it, so if he says, 'I am fasting tomorrow,' and he did not specify whether he is observing a fast of Ramadan, a time-specific vow, or a voluntary fast, it will be valid and account for that which is due.

Secondly, there is another category in which it is conditional to intend in advance, before the breaking of dawn, and to specify it [i.e. the intention] for the fast one is observing:

1. making up a fast of Ramadan;
2. making up voluntary fasts one had invalidated;
3. the fast for the various atonements (*kaffārāt*);
4. an unspecified vow, such as his saying, 'If Allah Most High cures my ill relative or friend, then I owe Him the fast of a day,' and he is then cured; or his saying, 'I hereby owe Allah the fast of a day.'

In all of these categories, the timing of the intention is from just after sunset until just before the break of dawn, so it must occur during this time. It is also necessary for one to specify the type of fast one is observing, whether it is the make-up of a fast of Ramadan, a voluntary fast one has nullified or a fast for atonement. Therefore, if one does not intend to fast from the night, or does not specify the fast one intends to observe, one's fast will not account for that which is due, but will instead be considered a voluntary fast.

CHAPTER THREE
Legal Rulings Pertaining to Fasting

THINGS THAT DO NOT INVALIDATE THE FAST

1. If someone fasting eats, drinks or has intercourse with his wife, while forgetting he is fasting, because of his saying ﷺ, 'If one eats forgetfully, then it is only nourishment which Allah has sent to him'; and his saying ﷺ, 'Whoever forgetfully breaks his fast during the month of Ramadan does not have to make it up, nor atone.'

   This ruling pertains to someone who remembers his fast after having finished eating, drinking or having intercourse. As for someone who remembers while doing so, then he has to refrain immediately; if he does not, his fast will be invalidated and it will become necessary for him to make it up.

   If the one fasting is a frail old man—or someone for whom the same ruling applies, such as a sick youth who is unable to fast—and we see him eat forgetfully, then it is better not to remind him, until he is satiated, out of compassion for him. As for when he is [seen as being] fit to fast till sunset without hardship, then it is necessary upon us to remind him immediately.

2. Application of eye drops or antimony (*kuḥl*) to the eyes, even if the one fasting tastes the drops or antimony upon his tongue.

3. If one has blood drawn through cupping, backbites, or intends to break the fast but does not.

4. If smoke enters one's throat inadvertently, it will not break his fast, though if one deliberately inhales smoke, it will break his fast.

5. If one smells a rose, a flower, perfume or musk. As for incense (*bakhūr*), its ruling is that of smoke: if it enters his throat inadvertently, it will not break his fast, while if it enters because of him deliberately inhaling, it will break it.

6. Dust from a mill, or the dust that scatters due to sweeping or during building work, is necessary to avoid for one's health and the validity of one's fast. If any of the aforementioned enters one's body cavity unintentionally, while trying to avoid it, the fast is not nullified.

7. The extraction of molars and teeth, and the application of medication over them, if blood or medicine does not reach the body cavity.

8. All types of injections, whether intramuscular or intravenous, prescribed by doctors as treatment. If it is possible to delay taking an injection that enters the bloodstream till the evening, then it is better to do so.

9. If one wakes up in the morning in a state of major ritual purity, whether due to having had a wet dream or due to intercourse, prior to the adhan of *fajr* and reaches dawn while still in that state of impurity, or one sleeps during the day and wakes up after having had a wet dream. The state of major ritual impurity does not affect the validity of the fast, though one should hasten to wash oneself to perform the prayer—which is more important than the fast in the sacred law as it is the foundation of the religion, and its place in the religion is like that of the

head in relation to the body. Our master Muhammad ﷺ said, 'The pact which is between us and them is the prayer, so whoever abandons it has become a disbeliever.' (Narrated by Aḥmad, Abū Dāwūd, al-Nasā'ī and al-Tirmidhī who said that is well-to-rigorously authenticated (*ḥasan-ṣaḥiḥ*).)

One also hastens to wash oneself in order to remain energetic and clean, and so that the angels are not driven away from one. It is narrated by ʿAlī ibn Abī Ṭālib ؓ from the Prophet ﷺ, who said, 'The angels do not enter a house in which there is a picture, a dog or a person in major ritual impurity.' (Narrated by Abū Dāwūd, al-Nasā'ī and Ibn Mājah.)

Al-Bazzār narrates with a rigorously authenticated chain that Ibn ʿAbbās said, 'There are three people whom the angels do not approach: the one in major ritual impurity, the drunkard and the one anointed with *khalūq*.'[36]

10. Swimming and bathing, even if water enters the ears.

11. Swallowing phlegm, though one should ideally spit it out as it breaks the fast according to Imam al-Shāfiʿī.

12. Being compelled to vomit, even if it is a mouthful. As for someone who deliberately induces himself to vomit, then his fast is invalidated if it is a mouthful, but not if it less than that because of his saying ﷺ, 'Whoever is compelled to vomit when he is fasting, it is not incumbent upon him to make up [the fast]; if he deliberately induces himself, then let him make it up.'

    The same ruling applies to someone who in the morning while fasting tastes the acidity of acid reflux which he then swallows: it does not invalidate the fast if it is less than a mouthful, nor is the fast invalidated if it [inadvertently] returns back to his body cavity, whether it is a small or a large amount [i.e. a mouthful]. If he swallows what may remain in between his teeth from the remnants of the pre-dawn meal (*suḥūr*)

[36] A type of perfume that was used by women to rub onto the face.

or supper—while it is less than the size of a chickpea, or he swallows it without the assistance of saliva—then it does not invalidate his fast.

13. Suppositories administered through the genitalia of a man (his urethra) do not nullify the fast, as opposed to a woman.
14. Insertion of earbuds even if done so repetitively.

THINGS THAT INVALIDATE THE FAST, AND NECESSITATE MAKING IT UP WITHOUT REQUIRING ATONEMENT

1. Swallowing something repulsive that reaches one's body cavity, or something which has no nutritional benefit, such as eating dry uncooked rice, dough, flour, swallowing a date seed, cotton, one's saliva if its colour has changed to green or yellow, a pebble, iron, copper, gold, silver, soil or stones, and so forth.
2. Eating or drinking accidentally or through coercion, such as inadvertently swallowing rain, snow or hail after it enters one's mouth, or water when gargling or taking it up the nose [during ablution]; or if someone pours water down one's mouth when asleep.
3. Eating, drinking, or having intercourse with one's wife intentionally, after first having done so forgetfully.
4. Suppositories: anal, nasal and ear, including the use of nasal sprays.
5. A man who intends to fast from the night and then sets off on journey, and the dawn breaks while he is still travelling; he then intends to stay [as a resident for fifteen days or more] and eats after making the intention to stay. His eating is considered unlawful, and it is obligatory for him to make up the fast, without atonement.
6. A man who is a resident, intending to fast at the time of dawn break, but then sets off on a journey and eats while he is

travelling outside his city—it is incumbent upon him to make up the fast and he is considered sinful.

7. Someone who eats, drinks or has intercourse while he has doubt over the dawn break (i.e. it is not clear to him as to whether dawn has broken, while in reality it had)—it is incumbent upon him to make up the fast [when he realises the truth].

8. Someone who breaks the fast after being reasonably [more than seventy-five per cent] sure that the sun has set, and it then becomes apparent that it had not, it is incumbent upon him to make up the fast. However, if he merely doubted and was not reasonably sure, then by breaking the fast, he would be obligated to make up the fast and atone. Doubt, therefore, is not sufficient to exempt one of atonement, in this case, as there is certainty in the remainder of the day, and it is not removed by doubt as opposed to the previous case, where there was certainty in the remainder of the night.

9. Someone who induces himself to vomit, when it is [the amount of] a mouthful, because of his saying ﷺ, 'Whoever induces himself to vomit deliberately must make up the fast.'

10. Someone who eats that which emerges from between his teeth during the day if it is the size of a chickpea or bigger.

11. Someone who falls unconscious, even if he remains unconscious for the entire month of Ramadan; likewise someone who sleeps for a number of days. However, he does not make up the day in which he fell unconscious or asleep because the condition for the fast, which is the intention, exists, in which case if he was certain of not having an intention, he will be obliged to make up that day.

12. Someone who suffers from insanity for a number of days or a portion of the month. As for someone whose insanity continues for an entire month, even in terms of legal judgement (*ḥukm*), such that he regains consciousness at night or at daytime after

the time for the intention expires, he does not have to make it up.

Important note

Whosoever's fast is invalidated, even due to a valid excuse, which then ceases to exist, such as a person who eats accidentally or through coercion, it is necessary for him to abstain [from eating] for the remainder of that day, and that is out of reverence for the time of fasting: '*And whosoever venerates [all that is ordained as] Allah's waymarks, truly it is out of the God-consciousness in the hearts*' (Qur'an 22:32).

Likewise, a woman during menses or lochia, if she becomes ritually pure[37] after dawn break or during the day, it is necessary for her to abstain [from eating, drinking and sexual intercourse] for the rest of the day, even though it is necessary for her to make up that day.

A traveller, if he intends to reside [fifteen days or more], or returns to his city from his journey, after dawn or during the day, it is necessary for him to abstain for the rest of the day [even though it is necessary for him to make up that day].

Likewise, if a sick person recovers from his illness, or an insane person regains sanity, or a child reaches puberty after dawn or during the day, it is necessary for each of these to abstain for the rest of the day just as it is incumbent upon them to make up the fast, except for a child who reached puberty or a disbeliever who became Muslim after dawn, for they were not legally responsible prior to reaching puberty and accepting Islam, respectively. This is contrary to the case of the prayer, where it is necessary to make it up if one reaches puberty[38] or one becomes Muslim during its time.

---

[37] Namely, her menses or lochia cease and she thus becomes pure following a purificatory bath (*ghusl*).

[38] Legally speaking, one is considered to have reached puberty upon having a wet dream (whether a boy or a girl), or the release of menstrual fluid in the case of a girl, or by reaching fifteen lunar years of age without any of the aforementioned signs (for either a boy or a girl). ʿĀbidīn, ʿAlā' al-Dīn. *al-Hadiyyah al-ʿAlā'iyyah*, 31.

THINGS THAT INVALIDATE THE FAST, AND REQUIRE ATONEMENT IN ADDITION TO MAKING IT UP

If a legally responsible individual who is fasting (having made the intention from the night to observe Ramadan) does any one of the following things deliberately, without duress or forgetting (since someone who forgets, his fast is not invalidated at all), and not accidentally (since someone who breaks it accidentally has to make it up without the obligation to atone), while nothing unexpectedly befalls him afterwards which allows him to break the fast, such as illness, or before it, such as travelling—then it is incumbent upon him to make up the fast and atone.

1. Whoever consumes something in Ramadan which is customarily taken for nutrition or something similar, such as medicine, because a sound disposition induces one to take medicine for the well-being of one's body, or something that one would incline towards, such as eating, drinking, consuming raw meat, swallowing rain, snow, hail or a small quantity of salt.
2. Intercourse, whether or not one ejaculates, for both parties.
3. Smoking, in all its forms.

Whoever does any [one] of the aforementioned things, it is incumbent upon him, firstly to make up the fast, which is to repeat the fast of the day (s) he broke within the month of Ramadan, and secondly to atone. An atonement is a penalty due to his contravening a requirement of the fast [of Ramadan], and it is of various degrees:

1. Emancipating a slave: if one is unable to emancipate due to not possessing one, not having the money to do so, or there not being one, he then discharges the second obligation,[39] which is fasting;

---

[39] It then becomes obligatory to do the second (i.e. there is no choice to fast two months if one is able to free a slave, and likewise, one cannot feed sixty poor people if able to fast).

2. Fasting two consecutive months, in which neither the days of Eid or *Tashrīq*[40] occur; nor days in which the fast is broken for any reason, except menses, as that will disrupt the continuity [of the fast] and obligate one to reinitiate the fast, the exception being menses—its recurrence does not disrupt continuity;

3. If unable to fast two consecutive months, one can either feed sixty poor people two satiating meals—lunch and dinner, or two lunches, or two dinners, or a dinner and a pre-dawn meal—on the condition that those whom he feeds the second meal are the ones he fed the first meal. If he feeds a single poor person two satiating meals for sixty days, it is valid, and [likewise] if he gives every poor person half a *ṣāʿ* [two kilograms][41] of whole wheat or flour, or one *ṣāʿ* [four kilograms] of dates, barley or raisins, or he gives the equivalent value [in money, for instance] of two kilograms of wheat or four kilograms of something other than wheat [i.e. dates, barley or raisins].

Note

Whoever repeatedly breaks a fast without a valid reason, a single atonement will suffice if it occurs after the numerous broken fasts, even if the days in which he broke the fast were in more than one Ramadan. If, however, he breaks a fast by something that requires atonement and he then atones for that, and thereafter continues to break another fast, a second atonement becomes incumbent upon him, since he was not deterred by the previous atonement.

---

[40] The 11th, 12th and 13th of Dhū al-Ḥijjah: traditionally, the three days when the meat sacrificed during hajj would be left out in the sun to dry, which is when one should abstain from fasting.

[41] Half a *ṣāʿ*: a *ṣāʿ* is a traditional measure of volume equivalent to approximately 2.03 litres. It was customary for foodstuffs to be measured by volume previously and not by weight. One *ṣāʿ* equals 4 kg in weight.

THINGS THAT ARE SEVERELY OFFENSIVE FOR SOMEONE FASTING

1. Tasting something without it reaching one's body cavity, because it exposes his fast, even if voluntary, to becoming invalid.
2. Chewing gum which has no flavour and nothing of it reaches one's body cavity. However, if it has flavour or something of it reaches the body cavity (as happens with gum commonly chewed in our time), it will invalidate one's fast, and it is considered, when not fasting, severely offensive for men, because of the imitation of women therein, except if done in isolation when there is a need for it (such as removing bad breath).
3. Sexual contact without penetration is offensive if one is not confident in himself [i.e. in it leading to intercourse or ejaculation]. Some scholars have said that it is unconditionally offensive [whether one is confident in oneself or not] because 'whoever drifts close to someone else's sanctuary is on the verge of falling into it.'[42]
4. Intentionally collecting saliva in one's mouth and then swallowing it.
5. Anything that one believes will weaken one from continuing the fast (such as blood-letting, cupping and strenuous labour) because it exposes one's fast to becoming invalid.

THINGS THAT ARE NOT OFFENSIVE FOR SOMEONE FASTING

1. For a woman to taste food if her husband is ill-natured, such that he gets angry merely by there being too much or too little salt in his food. Likewise, for a man to taste food if he fears being deceived when buying [food], and similarly someone employed

---

[42] A reference to a hadith narrated by both al-Bukhārī and Muslim, encouraging the avoidance of doubtful matters.

to purchase [food] if he knows his boss is bad tempered, on the condition that none of these swallow anything they taste.

2. Applying oil to the moustache, antimony or perfume, smelling flowers and perfume, blood-letting and cupping if they do not weaken one from fasting.

3. Brushing one's teeth using the tooth-stick (*siwāk*), even if moist or at the end of the day, because of his saying ﷺ, 'The best trait of someone fasting is brushing with the tooth-stick.'

4. Gargling and taking water up the nose, even if they are done for other than ablution.

5. Having a bath and wrapping oneself with a wet garment with the intention of cooling oneself and warding off heat in order to invigorate oneself to complete the act of worship.

6. Kissing and sexual contact while confident in it not leading to ejaculation or intercourse.

CHAPTER FOUR

Extenuating Circumstances

Extenuating circumstances are: illness, travelling, coercion, pregnancy, breastfeeding, [extreme] hunger, severe thirst and decrepitude.

It is permissible to break the fast for:

1. Someone who, while ill, fears an increase in his illness [by fasting], or he fears delay in recovery, by being informed by a skilled upright Muslim doctor, or through past experience;
2. A soldier who knows with certainty or reasonable surety [from past experience], when being confronted by the enemy, that by fasting he would become too weak to fight;
3. A pregnant woman or a wet nurse if she fears mental impairment, death or illness, whether her fear is for herself or for her baby [whether by lineage or fosterage]. She is allowed to take medicine if a doctor informs her that it will help prevent diarrhoea for the suckling baby;
4. Someone who experiences severe thirst or hunger, fearing from it death, mental impairment, or loss of one of the senses, provided it was not due to him exhausting himself, because if it had been, an atonement would become incumbent upon him;

5. A traveller if he sets off on a journey before dawn, since it is impermissible for him to break the fast after having been a resident at dawn break. A traveller's fast, however, is more beloved to Allah if it does not pose any harm to him, due to the Most High's saying, '*And for you to fast is better for you.*' This is if the majority of his travelling companions are fasting, or are contributing towards the travel expenditure; if they are contributing but not fasting—or they are not fasting nor contributing—it would be better for him not to fast so that he may conform with the rest of the group;

6. A decrepit man (deteriorating in health day by day till he dies), a decrepit woman or any chronically ill person, even if young. It is incumbent upon all of these to give *fidyah*, and its amount is two kilograms of wheat or its value, for each day. They have the option to give it away either at the beginning of the month or at the end, and it is valid to give it away even to a single poor person. Whoever is unable to give *fidyah* due to poverty should seek pardon and forgiveness from Allah Most High;

7. It is permissible for someone observing a voluntary fast to break it due to a valid dispensation (which includes being a guest) from morning to noon (*zawāl*).[43] As for after this [time], it is impermissible, except if invited as a guest by one's parents, up until late-noon (*ʿaṣr*) if one fears it will offend them. If a person swears an oath that he will divorce his wife if So-and-so, who is fasting, does not break his fast, then the relied-upon position is that he breaks his fast even if it is a make-up fast of Ramadan—though not if it is a fast of Ramadan during the month—and he does not allow him to break his oath out of consideration for his brother's right.

---

[43] Just after the sun reaches its zenith, at the time of *ẓuhr*.

Point of benefit

It has been related in a hadith, 'Whoever breaks a fast for the right of his brother, then the reward of a thousand days of fasting is registered for him, and whenever he makes up [such] a day, the reward of two thousand days is registered for him.'

If someone observing a voluntary fast breaks it for whatever reason, it is necessary for him to make it up. And it is incumbent upon someone who breaks a fast due to the aforementioned extenuating circumstances to make up the fast after the circumstance has ceased. It is not conditional to consecutively make up the fasts, though it is recommended to do so and not to delay beyond the time of one's ability [to make them up], hastening towards good and absolving oneself of accountability. Whoever dies before the cessation of such an extenuating circumstance is not required to leave a bequest for the atonement of the fasts he broke.

1. Case scenario: a man becomes ill during Ramadan and breaks his fast because he is incapable of fasting, and then dies before recovery. There is nothing incumbent upon him. If [however] the extenuating circumstance ceases, he makes up those fasts he is able to. If he does not make them up, then leaving a bequest becomes incumbent upon him for the duration of those days he was a resident after travelling, and healthy after being ill and the cessation of the excuse.

2. Case scenario: a man was a traveller and so he did not fast during his journey for seven days. He then returned to his city in the evening of the first day of Eid ul-Fitr and remained resident therein for three days and then died. Such a person leaves a bequest for the payment of *fidyah* for three days only. If the following Ramadan comes and he has not yet made up what is incumbent upon him, or he began but did not finish doing so, he gives precedence to fasting the current Ramadan before making up the missed fasts, and there is no penalty for such a delay.

CHAPTER FIVE

Recommended Acts While Fasting and Ṣadaqah al-Fiṭr

1. Intending [to fast] at night, and to comply with the command of Allah Most High.

2. Abstaining from what Allah has prohibited, as fasting is not mere abstinence from food and drink; rather, it is incomplete without by lowering the gaze and guarding the tongue from backbiting, lying, swearing and insulting. Al-Bukhārī and others narrate from him ﷺ, who said, 'Whoever does not abstain from false accusation and acting in accordance with it, then Allah is in no need of him abstaining from food and drink.'

3. Not wasting his spare time during the day by playing games, cards and other such things. He should rather occupy his time with reading the Qur'an, remembrance [of Allah] or invoking blessings upon the Prophet ﷺ. Al-Ṭabarānī narrates from him ﷺ that he said, 'The one who remembers Allah in Ramadan is forgiven, and the one who asks Allah during it is not disappointed.' If one becomes bored, one should sleep a little because the sleep of someone fasting is considered an act of worship, his silence is glorification, his deeds are multiplied and his supplication is answered.

Playing backgammon is impermissible outside of Ramadan, then what about in Ramadan? It is likewise impermissible without betting, though when it is accompanied by betting, even if it be with something small (such as a packet of sugar), it is unlawful because it is considered gambling.

4. Hastening to break the fast when he is certain the sun has set. It is not permissible for him to rely upon his watch, nor upon the cannon[44] because the watch may be incorrect, and likewise the cannon.

   There is an issue here one should pay heed to: some smokers take a draw or two of a cigarette just before sunset, considering it insignificant, despite the fact smoking a cigarette is the same as eating or drinking. Thus, if one deliberately takes a draw and inhales it before sunset, even if by a minute, one's fast is invalidated and it is incumbent upon one to make it up and atone.

5. It is recommended for someone fasting to supplicate when breaking the fast. Al-Tirmidhī and others narrate the hadith of Abū Hurayrah ﷺ that the Messenger of Allah ﷺ said, 'There are three [people] whose supplication is not rejected: the one fasting until he breaks fast, the upright leader, and the supplication of the oppressed.' It is from the Sunnah to say,

اللَّهُمَّ لَكَ صُمْتُ وَبِكَ آمَنْتُ وَعَلَيْكَ تَوَكَّلْتُ وَعَلَى رِزْقِكَ أَفْطَرْتُ وَصَوْمَ الْغَدِ
مِنْ شَهْرِ رَمَضَانَ نَوَيْتُ فَاغْفِرْ لِي مَا قَدَّمْتُ

Allāhumma laka ṣumtu wa bika āmantu wa ʿalayka tawakkaltu wa ʿalā rizqika afṭartu wa ṣawma l-ghaddi min shahri Ramaḍāna nawaytu faghfir lī mā qaddamtu.

'O Allah, for You I have fasted, and in You I have believed, and in You I have placed my trust, and with Your sustenance I break my fast; and tomorrow's fast of

[44] A cannon is sounded in some Muslim countries to mark sunset during Ramadan.

Ramadan I have intended, so forgive me for what I have done in the past.'

6. Not delaying the sunset prayer (*maghrib*) beyond its time. Some waste their time eating their meal upon breaking their fast, followed by using the bathroom, performing ablution, and then perform *maghrib* just before *'ishā'*—this is a grave error. It is better for one to break the fast with a sip of water or the like, perform maghrib, and then have one's meal after the prayer. If one wants to eat before performing the prayer, one should perform ablution before breaking the fast, so that when the time comes, he eats and gets up to perform maghrib without delay.

7. Not missing the prayer of *Tarāwīḥ*, as it helps in digesting food and invigorating the body, and is a cause for forgiveness of one's sins. It is twenty cycles of prayer in accordance with the practice of the Muslims, and the consensus of the Companions and those after them. Whoever denies it is a misguided innovator whose testimony is rejected, as it is a sunnah of Allah's Messenger ﷺ and his Companions after him. How could it not be the case, when he ﷺ said, 'Adhere to my Sunnah and the Sunnah of the rightly guided caliphs after me; hold on to it with your molars.' Al-Bukhārī, Muslim and others have narrated from him ﷺ, 'Whoever stands in prayer during Ramadan [i.e. for *Tarāwīḥ*], out of faith and anticipation [of reward from Allah], will be forgiven his past sins.' The prayer of *Tarāwīḥ* is the best act of worship one can perform during the nights of Ramadan.

8. Not missing the pre-dawn meal (*suḥūr*), which is the meal at the end of the night. He ﷺ said, 'Have your pre-dawn meal, for verily it is a source of blessing; have a pre-dawn meal, even if it be half a date.' Qāḍī 'Iyāḍ said, 'This blessing maybe spiritual (*ukhrawiyyah*),[45] which is the facilitation for the one having the pre-dawn meal to remembrance [of Allah], prayer and seeking

---

[45] *Ukhrawiyyah*: literally an ascription to the *Ākhirah* [afterlife].

forgiveness, or worldly, which is the strength to fast and do other daily activity.' He ﷺ said, 'Seek assistance from the pre-dawn meal in fasting during the day.' By virtue of the pre-dawn meal, one gains energy and resistance to bad character that is induced by hunger.'

9. To delay the pre-dawn meal and hasten in breaking the fast is recommended, after ascertaining the commencement of the time, because of his saying ﷺ, 'Three things are among the traits of the messengers: hastening in breaking the fast, delaying the pre-dawn meal and placing the right hand over the left in prayer.'

   Some may claim that eating food just before dawn may be harmful to one, though the blessings of the pre-dawn meal are attained even by drinking water. He ﷺ said, 'The pre-dawn meal is a blessing even if one of you was to drink a sip of water, for indeed Allah shows mercy to those who have the pre-dawn meal and the angels pray for them.'

   Whoever is unable to pray the *Tarāwīḥ* after '*ishā*' should pray it at the time of the pre-dawn meal, because it is valid up to the time of dawn.

10. Avoiding certain phrases uttered by laymen, such as the words 'Ramadan is a burden'; it is feared for someone who utters such words that he may have committed disbelief—we take refuge in Allah. Likewise, the words of some people when a guest arrives 'Ramadan is a miser', and similar phrases that the purified sacred law does not permit.

11. It is recommended to increase in charity because of what has been narrated by al-Tirmidhī, on the authority of Anas ؓ, that the Messenger of Allah ﷺ was asked, 'Which charity is the best?' to which he replied, 'Charity during Ramadan.'

12. It is recommended to give the one fasting something with which to break his fast. Al-Tirmidhī, Ibn Mājah and Ibn Ḥibbān all narrate from him ﷺ, 'Whoever gives the one fasting something

with which to break his fast will have the like of his reward without diminishing the reward of the one fasting in the slightest.'

13. It is recommended for him to exert himself in worship during the last ten days of Ramadan because they are the quintessence of the entire month. Aḥmad, Muslim and others narrate, 'He ﷺ would exert himself in the last ten days more than he would during the rest [of Ramadan].' Al-Bukhārī, Muslim and others narrate that when the ten would commence, the Prophet ﷺ would 'tie his sarong' (a metaphor for exertion in worship), and spend the night in worship, and wake his family up.

14. If he is able to perform *iʿtikāf*, he should do so, because he ﷺ would perform the *iʿtikāf* in the last ten days of Ramadan up until he passed away; then his wives after him would perform it.

    He ﷺ used to perform *iʿtikāf* in the middle ten days of Ramadan, and then Jibrīl عليه السلام came to him and said, 'That which you are seeking is ahead of you (i.e. the Night of the Divine Decree[46])', so he then performed the *iʿtikāf* in the last ten days of Ramadan. Ibn Masʿūd رضي الله عنه said, 'It can occur at any time during the year,' and the Greatest Imam [Abū Ḥanīfah] concurs, and it is stated in *al-Mabsūṭ*, 'The view of Abū Ḥanīfah is that it is

---

[46] There are numerous interpretations based upon the various possible meanings of the word 'al-Qadr': Al-Shirbīnī, in his *Tafsīr al-Qurʾān al-Karīm*, states, 'It is called the Night of the Divine Decree because Allah Most High apportions therein whatever matters He wills, such as death, lifespans, sustenance and so forth, till the coming year, which He entrusts to the angels Isrāfīl, Izrāʾīl, Jibrīl and Mikāʾīl (upon whom be peace).' He later says, 'The meaning of Allah Most High's apportioning the lifespans is that He reveals that to His angels and commands them to do that which is in their capacity, namely, recording for them that which He has decreed for that year, and acquainting them thereof. What is not meant is that He initiates [decreeing] on that night, because Allah Most High has decreed everything in pre-eternity before the creation of the heavens and the earth. It was said to Ḥusayn ibn al-Faḍl, "Has Allah not decreed everything before the creation of the heavens and the earth?" He replied, "Yes." He was asked, "So what is the meaning of the Night of the Divine Decree?" He replied, "Driving the preordained decrees to their appointed times and executing that which has been preordained." According to a weaker opinion, the meaning of 'al-Qadr' is constriction as the night is constricted by the sheer number of angels, like the one whose sustenance is restricted. It has also been said that it means honour, rank and nobility.' There are a number of other interpretations given, but those mentioned shall suffice.

in Ramadan.'[47] The majority of the scholars are of the opinion that it is in the final ten days of Ramadan. It has been related in a rigorously authenticated hadith, 'Seek it in the last ten, and seek it on every odd [night],' meaning that it may be the twenty-first, twenty-third, twenty-fifth, twentyseventh or twenty-ninth night [of Ramadan]. The majority of opinions state that it is the twenty-seventh night. Thus, every Muslim should be eager to spend the night in worship.

The Night of the Divine Decree has a great status. A man from the Children of Israel who carried arms (i.e. fought in the way of Allah) for a thousand months, was mentioned to the Messenger of Allah ﷺ, so he ﷺ wished that for his nation. Allah Most High thus gave him the Night of the Divine Decree, meaning, 'O Muhammad, indeed We have granted you and your nation in every year a night wherein whosoever does a good deed will have a reward that is better than the reward gained by that Israelite in a thousand months.'

THE SPIRITUAL RETREAT (*Iʿ TIKĀF*)

It means to stay in a mosque where the congregational prayers are held, even if the Friday prayer is not. A woman's retreat is in the masjid of her home, which is any room that she has designated to pray therein.

The spiritual retreat is of three types:

1. Necessary, which is a vow, such as one saying, 'I hereby owe Allah a retreat for three days.' Fasting is [also] conditional for its validity;
2. The communal emphasised sunnah, which is the retreat during the last ten days of Ramadan;
3. The recommended, which is to intend a retreat whenever one enters a mosque, since its minimal duration is but a moment.

---

[47] Both positions attributed to the imam.

The one in retreat cannot leave the mosque during the vowed retreat, or the retreat within the last ten days of Ramadan (this includes the woman in retreat at home), except for:

- a need countenanced by the sacred law, such as the Friday prayer and the two Eid prayers, in which case he leaves at a time that allows him to perform the prayer, along with its sunnahs,[48] and then returns. If he concludes [the remainder of] his retreat in the grand mosque, in which he performed the Friday prayer or the two Eids prayers, it would be valid, but nevertheless offensive;
- a natural need, such as urination, defecation, removal of impurities or taking a purificatory bath from major ritual impurity;
- an imperative need, such as the mosque collapsing, or to bear testimony in court when it becomes mandatory for him [in the absence of other witnesses], or he fears for himself or his belongings.

Such a person leaves his place of retreat on the condition that his departure is only so that he may retreat in another mosque. He must not busy himself along the way with anything else. If he leaves without any of the aforementioned excuses, such as going to his shop, visiting a friend, escorting a funeral procession (*janāzah*), or for anything else, and his retreat was:

- necessary, then it is invalidated and it is incumbent upon him to make it up;
- sunnah, then it is necessary for him to make up only one day;
- voluntary, then it ceases [at that moment], and there is nothing necessary for him to make up.

---

48 These are four cycles before and after the Friday prayer.

The retreat is also invalidated by intercourse and ejaculation through foreplay, even if done so absent-mindedly.

It is offensive for someone in retreat to bring an item for sale to the mosque, because it is as if he is treating it like a marketplace. It is also offensive to contract something for business, because he should be devoting himself to Allah Most High, so he should not busy himself with mundane affairs. It is also offensive for him to sell, or to vow silence, if he believes it to be an act of devotion, because they are prohibited due to their resembling the fast of the People of the Book.

A person should therefore speak well and about which there is an apparent benefit. He should guard his tongue from backbiting, tale-bearing, lying, drivel, and similarly those things in which there lies no benefit. This is emphasised with regard to both someone fasting and someone in retreat, since 'nothing is equal to safety'.

The etiquette of the spiritual retreat

The one in retreat should constantly be reciting the Qur'an, remembering Allah, invoking blessings upon the Prophet ﷺ, reading hadiths, studying sacred knowledge with others, and so forth.

It is recommended for every Muslim to spend the night of Eid in worship, such as standing in prayer, reciting the Qur'an, invoking blessings upon the Prophet ﷺ and remembering [Allah] at the end of the night.

Ibn Mājah narrates on the authority of Abū Umāmah ﷺ that the Messenger of Allah ﷺ said, 'Whoever stands in worship during the two nights of Eid (ul-Fitr and ul-Adha), anticipating reward from Allah Most High, his heart shall not die on the day that hearts die.' Some of the scholars have said that its meaning is that Allah will keep him steadfast in his faith at the time of the seizure [of his soul], and strengthen him when the two angels interrogate him in the grave and during the interrogation on the Day of Resurrection.

ṢADAQAH AL-FIṬR

It is necessary for every Muslim who possesses the *niṣāb*[49] (even if it is non-accruing; for instance, if he possessed an additional house or a plot of land whose value is equivalent to the *niṣāb*, *ṣadaqah al-fiṭr* would be necessary for such a person), even if a year does not pass with the amount [in his possession], and that is in surplus of his debts and basic needs (such as a house, car, home furniture and clothes).

A man discharges it on behalf of himself and on behalf of his nonpubescent children who do not possess *niṣāb*. If they do possess it, he may discharge it from their wealth. It is necessary for the grandfather to discharge the *ṣadaqah al-fiṭr* on behalf of his paternal grandchildren [if they are poor] in the absence of their father. As for his maternal grandchildren, he is not responsible for discharging it on their behalf.

A man is not responsible for discharging on behalf of his pubescent children or his wife, regardless of whether they are rich or poor, though it is better for him to do so if they are poor. Nor is he responsible for discharging on behalf of his parents, if they do not possess *niṣāb*, though it is better to do so.

Important points

1. Whoever is exempt from the obligation to fast, such as a sick person or a woman experiencing lochia, is not exempt from *ṣadaqah al-fiṭr*; rather, it is necessary to discharge it. They [the scholars] state, 'In discharging it there is acceptance of one's fast, success, salvation from the terror of the pangs of death and punishment in the grave.' The intention for it is required when giving it away, or when setting it aside from the rest of one's wealth.

---

[49] The minimum amount of wealth a person possesses obliging him to pay zakat: its amount is 85 grams (or 20 *mithqāls*) of gold; or 200 dirhams (700 grams) of silver. According to contemporary jurists, owning the monetary equivalent to the value of 85 grams of gold means an individual possesses the *nisāb* amount.

2. Someone who breaks the fast of Ramadan without an excuse is not exempt from *ṣadaqah al-fiṭr*, and similarly it is necessary for someone who neglects the prayer to discharge it.

3. The *ṣadaqah* of a wealthy minor or a wealthy insane person is discharged from their wealth. If it is not discharged on their behalf, it becomes necessary to do so after puberty or regaining sanity, respectively.

4. A wealthy woman is not responsible for discharging *ṣadaqah al-fiṭr* on behalf of her children, even if her husband is poor.

5. A man is not responsible for discharging *ṣadaqah al-fiṭr* on behalf of any stepchildren.

6. A widow is not responsible for discharging *ṣadaqah al-fiṭr* on behalf of her children, but if they have their own wealth, she discharges it from their wealth on their behalf.

7. It is commonly said by the laity that *ṣadaqah al-fiṭr* is a *riṭl*[50] of bread, which is in fact incorrect. It is only necessary to discharge the value of two kilograms of wheat, whether it be dirhams, cloth, sugar, rice, bread, or the like.

8. It is preferable to give *ṣadaqah al-fiṭr* to relatives, apart from one's parents, offspring and spouse. Hence a legally responsible does not give *ṣadaqah al-fiṭr* to his mother, father, grandparents, son, paternal grandchildren, or his daughter and her children, or his wife; nor does a wife give to her husband.

   The *ṣadaqah* can be given to one's brother or sister who are poor and to their children, a paternal uncle or aunt and maternal uncle or aunt who are poor and their children, and the rest of one's relations (since Allah does not accept charity from a person as long as there is amongst his relatives someone who is needy); then to one's neighbours, followed by the people of one's locality.

---

[50] Equivalent to 381.15 grams.

9. A person should give his *ṣadaqah al-fiṭr* to the poor people of his city or town, since it is offensive to discharge it to another city, unless there is a relative or a poor person who is needier therein. However, he should endeavour for it to reach the poor person's hand before Eid so that its wisdom is not lost.

   The amount of *ṣadaqah al-fiṭr* is two kilograms of whole wheat, or flour; or four kilograms of dates, raisins, barley or their equivalent value. If, however, it is a time of famine, then wheat, barley and anything consumable would be better than money, but if it is a time of prosperity, then money is better because of the various needs of the poor.

The time for its obligation

It is at the breaking of dawn on the day of Eid ul-Fitr; hence, *ṣadaqah al-fiṭr* is not necessary for whoever dies or becomes poor before dawn break.

Ṣadaqah al-fiṭr is not necessary for whoever becomes a Muslim or becomes [legally] wealthy after dawn break [i.e. he acquires the *niṣāb*] after dawn break.

If a mother gives birth to a child during Ramadan or on the night of Eid before dawn break, *ṣadaqah al-fiṭr* is discharged on the child's behalf, though if she gives birth after dawn break, then nothing is to be discharged on its behal.

Ṣadaqah al-fiṭr can be given in Ramadan, or just before or on the night of Eid. However, it is better to give it after dawn break on the day of Eid before the Eid prayer. It is offensive to postpone it until after the Eid prayer.

It is permissible to give numerous *ṣadaqah al-fiṭr*s to a single poor person, just as it is permissible to distribute a single *ṣadaqah* amongst numerous poor people.

CHAPTER SIX

The Secrets and Wisdom of Fasting

1. Forgiveness of one's sins and drawing near to Allah Transcendent and Most High.
2. The one who is fasting resembles the traits of the angels drawn near to Allah Most High, who do not eat and drink, or disobey Allah in whatever He orders them to do, but do as they are commanded.
3. The one fasting habituates himself to patience, steadfastness and order, since Muslims abandon food and drink in the morning at the same time, and break the fast at the same time.
4. Guarding one from falling into disobedience and sin.
5. Encouraging the rich to help the poor. Do you not see that a rich person, when beset by hunger, remembers the poor and needy, so his heart inclines towards them with compassion, mercy and assistance? The prophet of Allah Yūsuf عليه السلام had in his hands the treasures of the earth, in spite of which he would not eat until hunger became severe for him. When he was asked about it, he replied, 'So that I do not forget the hungry.'

6. Reducing intake of food and drink is a trait that has two benefits:

   - ignition of one's thought and the penetration of one's foresight, for the Prophet ﷺ has said, 'The one whose belly is hungry, his thinking is heightened and his heart is made sagacious.' Our master Luqmān said to his son while counselling him, 'O my dear son, when the belly is full, one's cognitive thought falls asleep, wisdom is muted, and the limbs are disabled from worship and purifying the heart';
   - it gives strength, health and energy. As some of them have said, 'The belly is the house of disease and dieting is the principal medicine.'

On this note, we should address what is incited by many ignoramuses that fasting is a cause for deterioration and weakness of one's health and body, and that the pre-dawn meal causes indigestion, swelling of one's eyes and gas, and such false insinuations. We want to remind the likes of these people that their neglect of the prophetic etiquette and manners has deprived them of attaining those wisdoms and splendid secrets. There is no doubt that someone who when breaking the fast, sits in front of the table in order to compensate for the two meals he missed during the day, and does not leave any room to breathe, delays praying *maghrib* till just before *'ishā'*, and then when the call for *'ishā'* is made, he prays *'ishā'* but not the *Tarāwīḥ*, then goes to his friend or relative's house to spend the night playing backgammon, backbiting and tale-bearing, and then when it is time for the predawn meal, he returns home to eat once again while his stomach has not yet digested the first meal—it is not long before this person, who has exhausted himself by spending the night awake and over eating, throws himself on the bed and sleeps until just before *ẓuhr* of the following day, abandoning the dawn prayer, and depriving himself of abundant benefits and magnificent blessings.

We have no doubt that whoever does the above will suffer deterioration in strength, weakness of body, indigestion and swelling of the eyes, because he eats in the same manner as livestock do, and is of those who disregard the etiquette of his Prophet ﷺ and the remembrance of his Lord.

As for the one who listens to the words of the Messenger ﷺ 'What a wonderful pre-dawn meal is dates', his words 'What a wonderful pre-dawn meal for a believer is dates', and his words 'The son of Adam does not fill a vessel worse than his stomach' and the indication in them to make the pre-dawn meal and the meal when breaking the fast a light one, so that they help him to fulfil the rights of Ramadan with which Allah has favoured the believers, that it may be a means of atonement for sins and emancipation from the fire, and they take admonishment from him ﷺ and be guided by his guidance—then this is the one who wins the pleasure of Allah and profits from his trade [i.e. rewards for his actions are multiplied]. The Messenger ﷺ has not encouraged us to take a pre-dawn meal so that we may fill our bellies with food and drink, but rather to pray at night and find an opportunity to remember Allah Most High, glorify and magnify Him, pray *tahajjud*, recite the Qur'an, perform the dawn prayer and other acts of obedience. Allah has not legislated for us this compulsory hunger every year for an entire month except that each individual should achieve the spiritual, health and social benefits which the legislation of fasting contains.

It is appropriate for us to refer to what the Proof of Islam Imam al-Ghazālī ؒ has said in his discussion on the benefits of fasting:

1. Restraining the gaze and subduing it from excessively looking at anything blameworthy and offensive, and anything which preoccupies the heart and distracts it from the remembrance of Allah Mighty and Majestic;

2. Guarding the tongue from drivel, lying, backbiting, talebearing, obscenity, rudeness, disputation and arguing, and compelling the tongue to silence and busying it with the remembrance of Allah and the recitation of the Qur'an;

3. Restraining one's hearing from listening to anything offensive since 'whatever is unlawful to say is unlawful to listen to';

4. Restraining the remainder of the limbs from sinning, such as the hands and feet from offensive actions, and restraining the stomach from consumption of doubtful foods at the time of breaking the fast;

5. One does not consume an excessive amount of halal food when breaking the fast such that it fills his belly;

6. That one's heart, after breaking fast, is suspended and wavering between hope and fear, since one is unaware of whether one's fast will be accepted, and thus he maybe among those who are drawn near [to Allah], or will be rejected, and thus he may be among those who incur [Allah's] wrath.

Concluding remarks

Ramadan is a blessed month which Allah has made mandatory for the Muslims to fast, their laity and elite, their rich and poor, for the benefits that they can reap. So whoever answers this call has won and succeeded, and whoever turns his back has failed and lost out. We seek from Allah success and sincerity, in words and deeds, for verily He has full power over that which He wills, and most worthy in answering [one's prayers]. May Allah send His blessings upon our master Muhammad, his family and Companions, and give them peace.